James P. Stanco

Utilizing the Strategic Marketing Organization: The Modernization of the Marketing Mindset

Pre-publication
REVIEWS,
COMMENTARIES,
EVALUATIONS . . .

"**J**ames Stanco's latest book, *Utilizing the Strategic Marketing Organization*, is excellent for anyone involved in marketing, whether it be a product, a service, or one's self.

Not unlike the works of Tom Peters or Jack Trout and Al Reis, Stanco takes a totally irreverent and cynical posture and effectively gets his point across–that today's organizations *must* market effectively if they are to succeed.

Utilizing the Strategic Marketing Organization is not only must reading for any student of marketing, but for those who are currently working in the field as well. In short, it is an excellent effort and a highly recommendable book."

Robert Janetschek
Director of Marketing,
Schiapparelli Biosystems, Inc.,
Fairfield, NJ

"This is a clearly written, step-by-step, real world book that offers total business solutions to a broad range of business clients. It will be of significant value to all corporate decision makers who are responsible for the continued profitable growth of their companies.

This book is also of critical importance to all start-up operations and privately held small to medium size companies. The Small Business Administration, along with the financial institutions that are involved in the financing of these businesses, should make this book mandatory reading before a financial commitment is made. I suspect that the annual failure rate of many companies could be significantly reduced by following the strategic steps outlined in this book."

George C. Perris
President,
Sierra Marketing Group,
Rocklin, CA

"In *Utilizing the Strategic Marketing Organization,* Mr. Stanco has taken an important step forward with an intelligent statement about marketing relationships that will work. He provides the rationale and a useful framework for implementing a genuine marketing plan within an SMO partnership. Since it is very difficult for most companies to see themselves as their customers see them, an objective but committed partner is essential. Mr. Stanco is very convincing that the partner must be a strategic marketing organization.

It's a new way of doing business and readers may find some of the concepts uncomfortable, but original ideas are like that. Mr. Stanco addresses every objection that a company might have about this new type of relationship, and provides step-by-step examples of how to find and work with a strategic marketing organization."

David L. Williams
Director of Sales and Marketing,
Axon Systems, Inc.
Hauppaugge, NY

More pre-publication
REVIEWS, COMMENTARIES, EVALUATIONS . . .

"*Utilizing the Strategic Marketing Organization* is an invaluable tool for anyone involved in 'growing' a business. Mr. Stanco's book is a complete guide to its subject. It not only describes the modern strategic marketing organization, but also distinguishes it from other service providers, and spells out how an SMO can help today's businessperson.

With this book, a reader has a seasoned marketing professional at his or her side. Using a down-to-earth style, the author provides solid advice on how to locate and work successfully with an SMO to accomplish business objectives.

Important information is presented in a concise, comprehensible manner. For example, one chapter leads the reader through an assessment of specific marketing needs, helping him or her to accurately define business requirements prior to seeking the assistance of an SMO. This material helps one save time, energy, and money, as well as avoid aggravation! In addition, the text includes detailed scenarios that illustrate how an SMO operates in two common business situations:

a new company launch and a product expansion effort. I recommend this book to anyone interested in marketing: business professionals, marketing instructors or students, writers, and designers. All will gain a better understanding of the strategic marketing organization's role in business."

Irene M. Peake
*Freelance Writer
and Communications Consultant,
Great Neck, NY*

"*F*inally a common sense approach to marketing for people at all corporate levels. Easy-to-read, easy-to-understand, easy-to-get-started. A breath of fresh air in a difficult world. Every chapter is filled with useful ideas."

David Stillman
*President, Global Exchange,
Smithtown, NY*

The Haworth Press, Inc.

Utilizing the Strategic Marketing Organization

The Modernization of the Marketing Mindset

HAWORTH Marketing Resources
Innovations in Practice & Professional Services
William J. Winston, Senior Editor

New, Recent, and Forthcoming Titles:

Long Term Care Administration: The Management of Institutional and Non-Institutional Components of the Continuum of Care by Ben Abramovice

Cases and Select Readings in Health Care Marketing edited by Robert E. Sweeney, Robert L. Berl, and William J. Winston

Marketing Planning Guide by Robert E. Stevens, David L. Loudon, and William E. Warren

Marketing for Churches and Ministries by Robert E. Stevens and David L. Loudon

The Clinician's Guide to Managed Mental Health Care by Norman Winegar

Framework for Market-Based Hospital Pricing Decisions by Shahram Heshmat

Professional Services Marketing: Strategy and Tactics by F. G. Crane

A Guide to Preparing Cost-Effective Press Releases by Robert H. Loeffler

How to Create Interest-Evoking, Sales-Inducing, Non-Irritating Advertising by Walter Weir

Market Analysis: Assessing Your Business Opportunities by Robert E. Stevens, Philip K. Sherwood, and J. Paul Dunn

Selling Without Confrontation by Jack Greening

Persuasive Advertising for Entrepreneurs and Small Business Owners: How to Create More Effective Sales Messages by Jay P. Granat

Marketing Mental Health Services to Managed Care by Norman Winegar and John L. Bistline

New Product Screening: A Step-Wise Approach by William C. Lesch and David Rupert

Church and Ministry Strategic Planning: From Concept to Success by R. Henry Migliore, Robert E. Stevens, and David L. Loudon

Business in Mexico: Managerial Behavior, Protocol, and Etiquette by Candace Bancroft McKinniss and Arthur A. Natella

Managed Service Restructuring in Health Care–A Strategic Approach in a Competitive Environment by Robert L. Goldman and Sanjib K. Mukherjee

A Marketing Approach to Physician Recruitment by James Hacker, Don C. Dodson, and M. Thane Forthman

Marketing for CPAs, Accountants, and Tax Professionals edited by William J. Winston

Strategic Planning for Not-for-Profit Organizations by R. Henry Migliore, Robert E. Stevens, and David L. Loudon

Marketing Planning in a Total Quality Environment by Robert E. Linneman and John L. Stanton, Jr.

Managing Sales Professionals: The Reality of Profitability by Joseph P. Vaccaro

Utilizing the Strategic Marketing Organization
The Modernization of the Marketing Mindset

James P. Stanco

The Haworth Press
New York • London

The Haworth Press, Inc., 10 Alice Street, Binghamton, NY 13904-1580

Library of Congress Cataloging-in-Publication Data

Stanco, James P.
    Utilizing the strategic marketing organization : the modernization of the marketing mindset / James P. Stanco.
        p.   cm.
    Includes bibliographical references and index.
    ISBN 1-56024-912-9 (hc.)
    1. Marketing–Management. I. Title
HF5415.13.S84 1995
658.8–dc20   95-6819
                                                                          CIP

Dedication

This book would not have been possible without a host of individuals who consciously or unwittingly made major contributions. Though they may maintain their innocence, insist they were duped, or deny any knowledge of this book, its author, or any association with either, I wish to thank the following individuals: Mrs. Bishop, my Ninth Grade English teacher who singlehandedly educated an entire generation of dense, flighty public school teenagers as to the wonders of language (presumedly English); my friend Tom Nozumi who gave me a chance to excel when no one else would; the late Jesse Wilkes who demonstrated that a creative marketeer could be vital into his 80s; Bill Gates who pioneered that magnificent machine; W. C. Fields who always gave suckers an even break; Dr. Edgar L. Gray who ignited a thirst for revision and review; J. Lyle McGuire whose treatment of Sam Spadowski is the best irreverent genre tale ever not created; Charles Dickens for saying it all; Muddy Waters and Howlin' Wolf for saying it plain and simple; Paul Walsh and Adam Strickland for the time, the energy, and the desire to do it right; Doggo for keeping me loose; Irene Peake whose offer to fearlessly wade through six-foot high piles of manuscript was real and appreciated; Bob Janetschek who encouraged at every turn; Bill Winston, the marketing wizard of the west, whose vision, energy, suggestions, friendship, and guidance were instrumental in this creation; and Sunny Sheppard who, after a constant bombardment of versions one through eight, can probably recite any given page verbatim, and without whom I would not have even attempted this task. Thank you, all of you. And to all a good night!

ABOUT THE AUTHOR

Mr. Jamie Stanco is the founder and President of Progressive Marketing Group, Inc., a Strategic Marketing Organization located on Long Island, New York. Mr. Stanco, who conceived, formulated, and coined the concept and term "SMO," draws on more than twenty years of experience in product and service marketing, corporate identification, public relations, technical and business writing, and advertising administration. Mr. Stanco is one of the exceedingly rare breed of creative marketeers equally at home with the conceptual and implementational realities of strategic and tactical marketing. As a recognized high-tech marketer, he has long been the primary creative marketing force for clients in a wide array of technical and consumer fields, as distinguished by repeat BOLI, APEX, and other awards.

Presently he is the managing editor of professional newsletters in several fields. The newsletters have received numerous marketing, graphics, and communications awards. Mr. Stanco has also headed strategic and tactical market research projects in telecommunications, precision optics, healthcare and medical electronics, semiconductors, computers, audio, radiology, business machines, music, musical instruments, copiers, and facsimile.

In addition to having numerous articles published in diverse publications, he is the author of a novel, *The CanCans of Canton.* He has served on the board of directors of two hi-tech electronics and communications corporations, and is a member of the American Management Association, the Biomedical Marketing Association, the National Trust, the L.I. Association, the L.I. Advertising Club, and the Theodore Roosevelt Association. Mr. Stanco also serves on the Editorial Advisory Committee for several Haworth Press publications.

As the prototypical SMO, Progressive Marketing Group, Inc. provides specific services to a select range of clients and organizations. Typically, such services include research and development, strategic marketing, tactical marketing, creative expression, and plan implementation. Though based in New York, the agency has provided counseling and direction to national organizations all over the U.S.A. and to clients in Japan and New Zealand.

CONTENTS

 # So You Need Marketing Help, Do You?

So you need marketing help, do you?

In 1492, when Columbus sailed the ocean blue as the old rhyme goes, it took him some 73 days to cross the great expanse known as the Atlantic Ocean and locate the New World. Today's SSTs can do that in 3.5 hours, transporting more goods and more people with far greater comfort (though the food is probably equally dismal). In most business circles of the Modern Age, this type of transition is termed "progress." And "progress" is almost always unilateral...just as we've made "progress" in fat-free cottage cheese and tactical nuclear weapons, we've also made "progress" in marketing, advertising, and promotion. In today's Modern Age, we market with our minds, not by blind faith, not with piles of meaningless data, not with esoteric plans upon plans upon plans, nor with new far-reaching philosophies so broad they're more nebulous than the watery abyss Columbus eventually crossed. And our minds give us a particularly enigmatic thought process called strategy. Today we market all types of goods and services with strategic precision. The organization that does market correctly succeeds, the company or individual that comes up short almost always fails. That was true in Columbus' day as well.

Today the staggering inability of so many to understand so little, the mind-boggling costs of the traditional, dyed-in-the-wool advertising agencies, the narrow-minded focus of the vaunted marketeers, the reams and reams of unrevealing documentation of the classic researchers, are being recognized for what they really are: products of a bygone era. Today is the age of the Strategic Marketing Organization or SMO. Columbus would be proud.

LET'S GET OUR
DEFINITIONS STRAIGHT

I don't need words, I need action!

How do you know you need marketing help?
It's very simple. The handwriting is on the wall. Except it's more glaring, a lot like graffiti. Sales are down, or stagnant. Your sales force is complaining that they need tools, leads, backup, etc. Telemarketers are reading *Robert E. Lee, Volume 3.* You've tried half-heartedly in the past to make an effective change, without any effect. The competition is thriving, judging by the frequency of their ads and direct mail which seem to appear everywhere, in areas that you are relatively certain are incorrect. Your professional society is abuzz with words you can recognize, spell, and comprehend, but whose actual meanings elude you. And you can't take the time away from being an owner/officer/CEO/partner/operator, etc., to learn what you need to know.

So how do you help your business? Get marketing help! When? Now! And that's where your task gets even stickier. You've got to know where to begin, let alone where to end up. In your field of expertise, whether it's medicine, engineering, accounting, manufacturing, distribution, etc., you know where you should wind up! Marketing is different. Concentrate on your core business. Leave marketing to the pros. So if you're going to hire someone or some firm to do this for you, make sure that they're the right ones. And make sure you consider an SMO.

What, you should be asking, is an SMO? This is not simple to explain. It's still a developing concept seeking fruition. The hand-writing is on the wall, but it's not completely finished. SMO stands for "Strategic Marketing Organization."

"Oh yes," the semi-learned masses exclaim, "an advertising agency."

Isn't SMO just another term for an ad agency?

No! Other names for ad agencies exist. They include:
a. Horse traders.
b. Super slick salesmen selling sand to the Saudis.
c. Magicians, sleight-of-hand manipulators, marketing pickpockets.
d. Poor dressers.
e. Insincere former used car salesmen.
f. @#$%&^!!
g. Pick any three. They all apply at times.

A Strategic Marketing Organization (SMO) is in many ways the antithesis of an advertising agency.

Ad agencies tip their hands in their own description of themselves...after all, if they're such great communicators, they can at least get what they do for a living correct, can't they? Like XYZ Advertising Co., Ltd., Inc., or Sitton McCann Advertising, Inc. What should we think that they do? Outfit scuba divers? Paint houses? So advertising agencies...advertise. Just like direct mail houses directly mail, and public relations agencies publicly relate.

The conceptual model of the SMO differs. An SMO's business is not the perpetuation of an advertising campaign or a direct mail program, or publicity, or any program...an SMO's business is the perpetuation of **your** business! As such the SMO must jump in, learn your business, be saturated with exactly what makes your products, your image, your company, your philosophy, —and how you — tick, work, function, succeed. And yes, an SMO might utilize advertising or direct mail or publicity to grow your business...and then again it might not. It's what you need that concerns an SMO, because they can provide customer-tailored services for virtually any situation. They don't have to sell you on advertising per se...or anything ...except what they envision will be the best plan to achieve goals...your goals, not their goals. And that's what this book is all about. Read on and learn a bit more about the Strategic Marketing Organization; in virtually every case, it will pay.

So really, what in tarnation is an SMO?

SMO stands for Strategic Marketing Organization. That and some loose change might buy you a cup of coffee, a few stamps, or possibly get you on the subway. The real question should be *"What does an SMO do that actually makes it an SMO?"*

OK. Keep explaining.

An SMO represents your total company from sea to shining sea...which in marketing terms means from your own sparkling pristeen self-image to the realities of your image/position/facade where it really counts...with your clients and vendors. The SMO incorporates product, service, image, and company. The starting point is before most other competitive marketing companies and individuals...and extends far beyond their horizons.

Then where does an SMO start and end?

At the beginning and the end. The SMO is characterized by incorporating five major segments within its structure. They are:

1. Essential Research & Development.
2. Strategic Marketing.
3. Tactical Marketing.
4. Creative Expression.
5. Implementation.

Don't consultants, agencies, and strategic marketers all do this?

Are you kidding?

Why isn't the term STMO (Strategic Tactical Marketing Organization)?

Because SMO is easier to remember? Because we do not spell particularly well? Neither. Because a tactical marketing, advertising, or promotional company is only concerned with immediate needs. Their vision is one of necessity. Others might call it tunnel vision...or putting out fires...or tending the sheep. So their marketing approaches and programs are similarly structured...for short-term results. They are usually completely focused on one goal...and so are their resulting programs. That's a bit shortsighted. Just ask the successful Japanese firms about a six-month marketing plan. Then hold your ears.

SMOs arrange and implement both long- and short-range planning. To an SMO, tactical marketing is included, but is only a part of "the big picture." So strategic in this case includes tactical...whereas tactical can never fully include strategic. Got it? And yes, SMO is easier to remember.

So why aren't the Madison Avenue Boys becoming SMOs?

Who said they are not? The trend is beginning to affect the big boys everywhere, including outside the USA. Except, as you might expect, the Fluff Street Fluffies might pump air into the SMO concept and label themselves "boutique agencies," "power branders," "creative factories," etc. In most cases, they are spinoffs or satellite shops. Their prime function is to "service the account" though in many cases, it's actually to "save the account" for the agency. All too often accounts (even large accounts) suffer from lack of the three i's...agency *interaction, initiative,* and *involvement.* The message should be clear: the SMO thrives on the three i's...and cannot function properly without them.

How can you state flat-out that advertising doesn't work?

Advertising **DOES** work. It just may not be the right answer for you. It **can be** a slice of the marketing pie, perhaps even the major piece. But by itself it is just as likely to be inadequate as the answer to your problems. Especially in business-to-business environments. If you consider that the advertising agency's chief skills are advertising...what does that tell you? That you can be relatively certain that any proposal will include advertising recommendations. Is this unprofessional? No. Unethical? Of course not. It is merely the mindset of such organizations.

The SMO is by nature a different mindset. The SMO considers all the needs and selects from all entrees on the menu, weighing every need, every possibility without artifice, without allegiance or partiality to anything...except the best strategic and tactical marketing programs for the client. Boutique schmootique. Where agencies are advertising agencies, you will receive as a major component in your program...advertising! Big surprise! It's like being on a low-fat diet, walking into a health food restaurant and ordering the "low-fat dinner special" and receiving a crisp fresh salad, a diet cola, and — surprise — a double cheeseburger with bacon, french fries, and a chocolate extra thick shake. You should know better. Always know what you're getting into with edibles and marketing plans! Don't accept a cheeseburger and the trimmings and let anyone tell you it's a low-fat diet. Get the value of what you've ordered. Sure, you can consume both meals, but the first is perfect for your health and the second could be deadly.

The fact is, most boutique agencies are merely smaller versions of bigger companies. Their efforts may be more targeted to your account...or maybe not...but that hardly guarantees a broad scope of initiative, of real time, hands-on research, creativity, execution, or management or professional involvement, or imaginative interaction. Get the real thing before your competitors do...get a real SMO.

So what's the r-e-a-l difference?

It's simple. Everything is simple if you get away from the bull, the chaos, the hype and open your business vault of a mind to consider something new and different. SMO is an essentially simple difference in mindset that affects intention...a simple difference in philosophy that affects your entire business...a simple difference in direction to create a clear window of operations...and a simple difference in dedication to create a better atmosphere to work in and breathe in. So an SMO differs in mindset...and it's your mind that has to be open. Vive la différence!

So how does an SMO differ from a marketing agency?

In a big way. Typically, marketing agencies deal with bringing a product or service to specific markets. They are not necessarily concerned with a company or the specific business goals of that organization. Also, it becomes increasingly difficult for true marketing companies as the number of products and/or divisions increase.

How does an SMO differ from a strategic marketing consultant?

In depth. In capability. In organization. An SMO encompasses the talents of a Strategic Marketing consultant. However, an SMO goes further, and is typically structured to **implement** the recommendations of the designated program. Typically, consultants are best off "consulting." Attempts at implementation are usually memorable, and not for positive reasons.

Isn't implementation a conflict of interest?

Not at all. Remember the conceptual model of the SMO demands that the SMO be totally saturated with the company, its needs, goals, abilities, drawbacks, shortcomings, etc. The concept of SMO **demands** complete involvement...which makes the SMO part of your company! And that's not a conflict of interest but a concurrence of interest.

Doesn't this conflict with account-side services, flexibility, and profitability?

Tunnel vision can have you focusing on the relationship from a job or departmental viewpoint...meaning that every news release or ad should be bid on by three different bidders, etc. That's 1960s-70s -80s mentality, "grab the lowest quote, screw the rest, get three more estimates next time." This does a few very negative things. It:

1. destroys the unified approach, creating a temporary and artificial partnership on each project. There is no loyalty being built. Very 1980s.
2. relegates every project to a "dollars-invested" basis, not a "dollars-recouped" basis. Short-sightedness rears its ugly head.
3. negates the ability of any one organization to be a vital, in-depth contributor to the client's overall positioning plan. The client then winds up with a patchwork marketing program...using odds and ends of several companies' services ...that may be far from the best quality services they have to offer...or endeavors to perform the tasks internally with less than adequate staffing.

4. makes the proposed positioning plan suspect to ulterior motives, a most dangerous scenario if it goes unrecognized.

Isn't an SMO just for privately owned firms?

Whatever gave you that idea? Certainly SMOs have the potential to function best in environments characterized by strong individuals who have the vision to see what is genuinely possible, the common sense to know an advantageous situation when they see one, and the courage to resist the pressures to hire:

a) new staff.

b) the boss' brother-in-law.

c) new staff that may be the boss' brother-in-law.

...and select the organization that can deliver you into the next century. If that's limited to private companies, then SMOs are only for private organizations.

How about a definition of an SMO in 50 words or less? How about 36 words?

An SMO is an organization wholly dedicated to its clientele that provides the research, the strategic process, the tactical plan, and the creative expression, and implements and executes the program via a single point of contact.

Wake up! Do the smart thing. You want to hire an organization to avoid all the pitfalls, cat calls, hidden snags, etc. Get an SMO. Why fall back into the same old trap?

But I need to save money.

Save money or make money? Either way put your efforts into something ultra-safe that will make you money...the SMO. Keep in mind that marketing requires investment. Which is why you need a plan and a position. Keep in mind that if an SMO coordinates your tactical promotional efforts from concept through implementation, **your** own strategic control is maximized. There's no passing the buck, no "don't look at me's," no chaos. The buck stops here. Always. You know the source and if the plan doesn't work to your expectations, that doesn't necessarily kill the concept of the SMO, it merely reflects on your specific choice of SMOs. So sharpen your interviewing skills. By assigning an overall budget and putting it in the correct hands of a worthy SMO, you're enfranchising the SMO to do something that's infinitely superior to what your marketing alternatives could do: put the right SMO people on the right specific job...without surrendering control...without one of your own marketeers breaking a fingernail...or a sweat. Save money? Make money? Get an SMO.

What about team spirit?

Esprit de corps? Are you afraid that they'll react negatively to an SMO horning in on their territory? It's possible. People are territorial. And protective. And envious. But mostly they are worried about their jobs. So be 100% honest with them up front.

Regarding team spirit, why would they react negatively? If you're certain that it's the right thing to do for the good of the entire organization, don't just enfranchise the staff...find out if their fears are valid. If not, and team spirit is affected, it sounds like you have the wrong people on your team.

2 How Does This Affect Me?

So do I need my inside marketing people at all?

This is a question that every executive will ask. Of course, it depends on the individual situation, but generally speaking yes, yes, yes! Just don't enfranchise them to produce what the SMO can produce better, more professionally, and in the long run, less expensively. Remember after staff time, salaries, benefits, etc., are figured in, the SMO's pricing seems downright attractive. No, give your marketing department the freedom to perform the functions they were hired for...to market your products/services in conjunction with your sales plan...and leave the real implementation to the implementators...your SMO.

I'm not sure I know my needs.

No one seeks marketing help without a need. As the old saw goes, *"If it ain't broke, don't fix it."* But you wouldn't be reading this if you didn't need marketing help (unless you're one of those bug-eyed datamaniacs who has a compulsive urge to digest every iota of information on some esoteric subject). You could be a physician or dentist who sees his patient load lagging...a retailer whose business is off 50% while your competition is up 20% or only down 10%...a distributor with lines no one knows...a manufacturer who believes in his product but can't seem to convince anyone else...or just about anyone in business today. Discover what you **need**, but not just what you would like...sales growth or increased profitability...presence at final bid time...enlarged market share...new product launches. Analyze, analyze, analyze! The bottom line is that you are need-driven...with a need and desire to increase and grow your business. So you recognize that you need marketing help. Now where do you go?

3

GETTING REAL:
LET'S PROMOTE
A JUNIOR PERSON

SCENARIO NUMBER ONE:

Route(s) to Travel

There are a number of time-proven routes to travel in what could easily seem like an endless search. Here are six scenarios that are common knee-jerk responses to the enigma that confronts your marketing for more and better sales. Read them. Try them on for size. Picture yourself in each scenario, smiling because you're thinking you've found the answer and won't have to read the rest of this book. Think again. And read on.

The setting: You're embarking on a new direction and you recognize that you need marketing help. Now what do you do?

Scenario Number One: "Let's promote a junior person."

This is the most typical knee-jerk reaction of all. Welllll...it is possible that this could work. It's also possible that the dinosaurs became extinct due to consuming bad nachos and salsa sold to them by little green alien invaders during the Jurassic Gold Rush. In other words, the likelihood isn't particularly great—so restrain yourself. Ask yourself (in private) if you actually believe that it's possible...that a junior person can research, design, troubleshoot, custom tailor, and implement a full-scale, real time, marketing program...one that's going to put you and your company over the top? Or should we say, are you willing to stake your business on that possibility? Or your reputation? In which case we have a few bridges and some swampland earmarked for your personal investment.

Junior people are juniors for good reasons...they cannot effectively do the job of a senior person. The most common reason is usually lack of experience. (Unless they are Peter Principled wherein they've risen to their own personal level of incompetence.) Do you really want them to make their fledgling mistakes on your time...your payroll...with the future of your business at stake? Many companies do just this...regardless of whether or not Mr./Ms. Junior Person is ready. Why would you do this? Examine the situation closely and **surprise**, you'll find that nearly everyone does it to save money. Do you really think it's wise to look to save money at the expense of the market expansion or sales growth or profitability that you are pledged to pursue? How much does saving money count vs. making money? Do you really think you'll save money in the end result when everything is judged?

Think of your investment in terms of time, equipment, supervision, etc. And potentially, you're denigrating what needs to be, by your own definition, a dynamic program that produces results. Remember too, that Mr./Ms. Junior Person will have to be replaced. It's one thing to promote from a backup role, but ironically, a promoted backup also needs...a backup...to cover what they were doing in the first place...with no drop-off in the productivity...unless they were just punching the clock and performing super menial tasks...in which case why would you make them responsible for vital marketing anyway? Whew!

There's more. Even if your nouveau-senior can implement most of the real day-to-day marketing as you need it, chances are you'll still need the services of non-marketeers...and idea person possibly...perhaps a writer or tech writer...and definitely a graphic designer...not just any one, of course, but one who's plugged into your market. Try to source that one out! So why not hire all three at once, in the form of an SMO?

Monet might have been a great impressionist, Frank Lloyd Wright designed many magnificent edifices, and perhaps no one could handle a brush better than Picasso...but you're going to need someone who can produce **what you know you need**, not someone who'll design what **they** want to design without regard for the real market. Pretty pictures are nice to look at, but they won't help your sales force or your bottom line. A good strategically conceived and implemented marketing program will. Get an SMO to do it for you.

Further (do you need further convincing?) with this promote a junior approach — you start to become your own business within a business. That's called empire building. It was wonderful for Charlemagne,. Alexander, Genghis Khan, etc., but they're all dead. So are Edison, Henry Ford, John Jacob Astor, Cecil Rhodes, and J.P. Morgan. So don't be an empire builder even by accident. You're a physician, a retailer, semiconductor manufacturer, computer consultant, dairy products distributor, electrical contractor, printer, etc. Your business **needs** marketing...but this way of proceeding **is not** marketing. Why spin your wheels? Cut to the chase and get going. Make yourself a promise. Don't get desperate. Don't promote the junior unless you can't locate a great SMO.

4 WE'LL EXPAND OUR MARKETING DEPARTMENT

SCENARIO NUMBER TWO:

We'll expand our Marketing Department

First of all, you have to have a marketing department to begin with, and that little factor eliminates some 50% of all the businesses in the USA and Canada. Second, you have to have the right mix of talented people, physical space, direction, technology, expertise, equipment, desire, follow-up, accountability, etc., in your base to build on. And then also, in a year or two, a dedicated (a modern synonym for "captive") marketeer can easily become a 9 to 5, clock-punching mouseketeer...or worse, a puppeteer as the proverbial times change and pass on by. Don't fool yourself. Expanding a marketing department is not a onetime investment, it's continual. Internal marketeers, even if they're willing to continue learning simply don't get the exposure and breadth of experience that external ones do.

The realm of the bean counter, the bottom line, also comes into play. Plug in your calculator and calculate the following: help wanted ads and/or headhunters...salaries, expenses, benefits, taxes...stir in healthy amounts of pensions, 401Ks, raises, and health insurance ...add a major dose of training...mix in a dash of moving expenses, travel expenses, retraining, etc., and you'll instantly recognize the real bottom line...somewhere out there in the stratosphere.

We haven't even discussed the other risks. Are the new people the right people? How can you be sure? Why do they want to leave where they are at? If they're not the right ones, what do you do with them? How will the rest of the marketing department react to bringing in an "outsider"? And remember, people are tough to find, easy to hire, and impossible to let go. "Hire Me Fire Me" doesn't apply here.

Marketing Department expansion may be a viable alternative in some cases. But why not consider another scenario? Why not locate a hired gun, a seasoned marketing bounty hunter, who has the track record of knowing or diving in and learning specific market niches like yours...and may in fact already know yours well...someone whose business it is to fulfill your business needs...someone who markets, creates, and implements rather than a permanent fixture sheriff who may know neither your business nor your business niche?

"Well, I'll make sure that I hire someone who knows my business," you might reply. Fat chance. Look at the trade press. Is it coincidence that everyone else is seeking the same person with the same credentials? Just what you need...a bidding war for a suspect position. Then, if he/she interviews well but doesn't know the nuances of your business, that validates the theory: The marketing department is getting bigger, perhaps even wider, but not necessarily better, or "leaner and meaner." And if he/she does know the specific nuances of your business like what you produce, how many, how you do it, your margins, etc., ask yourself "How is it that they do know these things?" Don't get paranoid, get an SMO. They'll be more dedicated in virtually every case.

5 THE SALES DEPARTMENT CAN DO DOUBLE DUTY

SCENARIO NUMBER THREE:

Sales Department? Double What?

"The sales department can do double duty."

Yet another tempting, but recognizably inferior idea. Whether your actual sales are above or below your projected sales forecast has nothing to do with making this a bad idea. Whether you have a sales forecast or not isn't important. Whether or not your sales force is one person or 100 people doesn't matter. What really matters is that in marketing, convoluted thinking **never** pans out as the helping hand or the panacea that you originally envision it to be. It cannot be such, by its very nature, essence, and definition.

Look at it this way. Your salespeople are there to sell. And you need sales. So why burden your sales force by having them do anything but sell? That's what they're paid for isn't it? Doing double duty is one thing. It can work for a week or two. But what makes you think that your most talented and effective salespeople will be good enough at tactical or strategic marketing to even avoid falling flat on their faces? Are you willing to put them up against your competition's marketing team? Does success in sales guarantee success in marketing? Absolutely not. Yes, rare individuals can adequately make the transition*...but you'll need more than mere adequacy if your business is to grow and prosper, especially over the long haul.

The transition from sales to marketing will be particularly arduous if your normal, day-to-day sales efforts are more of an order-taking nature. Good, effective marketing requires **proactive** not **reactive** thinking and actions...and there's simply no substitution for that kind of aggressive get up and go. Then too, no sales manager worth his/her salt truly wants to bother with anything that "takes my people out of the field or off the phone." So you're apt to get resistance there too. Unhappiness breeds like mosquitos in a stagnant pond. You don't need to be bitten. And finally, what successful salesperson would want to change what he/she is doing so well? Anyone who does want to change is probably less than a shining star...so why put a dim bulb in a position that demands a floodlight?

*It's true with any field. Harry Truman was a haberdasher, and none-too-successful at that...and yet he was arguably one of the twentieth century's better U.S. presidents.

So, what is the end result of this "double duty" avenue of thought? An overworked, less productive sales force, possibly disenchanted employees, and a marketing program that has more holes in it than Bonnie and Clyde. **DON'T DO IT!** Get an SMO!

6 DESKTOP PUBLISHING WILL CURE IT FOR US

SCENARIO NUMBER FOUR:

Ahh the Panacea!

"Desktop publishing will cure it for us."

And for some portion of your requirements, this will be true...but that's probably only 5 to 10% of the total requirements. Learn this now and save your money. That's the desktop dilemma.

Desktop publishing may be the buzzword of the business lunch, but it's almost always an expensive way to create more work for yourself. Ever hear of "work smarter not harder"? It makes sense. To pursue this route, you first have to acquire the right desktop system, a task only slightly easier than splitting the atom with an electric can opener and a cherry bomb. Forget about software. The modern dictionary defines "software" as a synonym for "recurring nightmare;" that's because they left "expensive, as in bottomless pit" out of the definition. And forget about multi-media. It's still sci-fi as far as you're concerned.

Next you'll have to reserve a few months while you check out the unbelievable amount of sources and prepare yourself for an endless array of sales videos, CD-ROMS, slides, brochures, and flip charts. Take out a second mortgage to pay for your system and you'll have to commit to a decision that will make or break your future. Then you'll need a person to operate the system (no, they don't run themselves). You will, of course, resist the tempting urge to hire a novice and have them "trained" (see mistakes of previous chapter). So you'll dig deeper into your pockets and pay for an experienced hand on the tiller or keyboard as it may be. Then you'll pull your hair out when they explain that "Phrenology 1-2-3 is a new program" or "I know version 2.0, not version 3.2." You'll also discover by divine intervention which service contract to enact and you'll quickly learn why it doesn't cover what just went down on your system. Then too, you'll find out what software your operator needs, probably on a weekly basis, to produce brochures, with the infinite potential to be greatly inferior to what an SMO can produce...not to mention innumerable price lists and data sheets in a wide variety of colors that won't produce an extra dime in sales.

It gets better. Operators of desktop systems are just that — operators, not marketing professionals and often they're not even artists. The really good artists/operators are already employed — by SMOs, agencies, and the likes. So regardless of what you produce, chances are very good that there is no marketing strategy or rationale to virtually any of it. Remember, **you need marketing**! Resist the urge to compound your initial mistake by bringing in a fine-sounding extraneous payroll gobbler like a technical writer or a media planner, etc. What business are you in anyway? Never ignore your core!

And if you have an MIS department, don't be surprised when they feel threatened and want to control the desktop system and its destiny. Just what you need. So how will the desktop route help you to do better business? It won't! What then, you might ask, is the point of this route? None! Especially when the typical SMO is already equipped with far more prodigious desktop systems than you've ever heard of. Let them stay up on the latest software version of "Woof-5.0," or the newest hardware. This avenue is a dead end without a rewarding beginning. But you'd be surprised how many very intelligent businessmen, professionals, financial analysts, engineers, managers, accountants, etc., even strategic marketing consultants, have insisted that this is the direction to take...but it takes six to 12 long, non-productive and costly months before they realize that the desktop route is taking them.

Remember all that glitters is not gold. Sometimes it's jello.

7 LET'S HIRE A NEW AGENCY

SCENARIO NUMBER FIVE:

Ad Follies

"Let's hire a new agency."

Close, but no cigar. What's the difference between the new agency and the old agency? New faces? So what. New portfolio? Who cares. Fancier presentations. Ho hum. How about a new way of doing business? Don't hold your breath.

Ad agencies, as discussed previously, are just what the name implies —agents who provide advertising. Who died and made them strategic marketing geniuses? No one. So what's that got to do with marketing? Very little. With strategic marketing? Less. For the small company, practice, or consultancy, particularly where budgets are proportionally allocated, you can count on the larger agencies being uniformly uninterested. Frankly, they can't afford to handle your account. Indeed, the smaller agencies and one-man shops can all create pretty pictures...but wait...to an extent so could the desktop graphic boppers or even your own in-house people, only with an agency it costs more up front. So you get nice brochures, ads, etc., that are reasonably likely to be professional in nature. They're probably modern. They probably make you look better than before...particularly if before there was nothing or, forgive us, something you did yourself. But do they actually tell your story? Reveal your true position? Get to the nitty gritty? Tell your tale in the ways your audience understands? Do they accurately reflect your commitment? Do they positively differentiate you from the rest of your competition?

If you've said "no" to these questions, skip the next paragraph. If you've said "yes" to any of these questions, you're in deeper trouble than you think...because "nice" brochures and ads are likely to be major parts of an advertising program...and minor parts of a successful strategic marketing program.

Tricked you! Don't miss the boat. Pretty picture types can be only as successful as the program that spawned them and they will have minimal success outside of the program. So you've spent money ...and what you still lack is a solid program and true marketing for your specific fields, applications, niches, etc. You still lack the savvy, know-how, expertise, the wealth of successful experience, the consultation, the exchange of thought, the "rule by reason" of strategic marketing, etc....not to mention the flexibility that's vital to creating a program, implementing it, and making it work. Settle for an agency...but only if you have exhausted every resource and can't locate an SMO.

How about a Strategic Marketing Consultant?

Scenario Number Six:

Consultant, Consult Thyself

"How about a strategic marketing consultant?"

How about a hot cherry pie with steam bursting from the delicate handmade crust...with no cherry filling?

How about a brand new Ferrari, exquisite continental styling, leather seats, the works...but no engine?

And finally, how about a check for a million dollars, made out to cash or even to your name...but no authorized signature?

Ahhh, such are the great ironies of life in these modern times. And they're accurate enough...because a strategic marketing consultant can be almost anything, from any background, with almost any level of expertise, and any level of field experience. Remember, no man or woman is an island. Such gurus have a tendency to isolate themselves from the very areas they need to be immersed in. Also, good, bad, or indifferent, consultants are all too often unfairly perceived as hireable/fireable commodities. Erase this type of warped thinking from your memory banks. You can't have a successful relationship with this mentality.

So why not use a strategic marketing consultant? If you don't know the answer already, you've been skipping pages and will not pass the pop quiz or the mid-term. A strategic marketing consultant? That's a fine solution, provided you're only looking to solve half a problem or receive half of the right answer. (And that assumes the consultant is good at what she/he does.) Remember always, the SMO is more than a consultant...the SMO is an organization that provides the strategic process, the tactical plan...then implements both from a single point of contact. Being staffed, equipped, and capable of implementation separates most SMOs from consultants. And what if they can provide the proper implementation? Wellll...maybe you're not dealing with a consultant per se...maybe you're already dealing with an SMO. **SO MAKE SURE!!** Jump into the fray and find out! Do they provide tactical services? Do they provide strategic plans? Do they implement programs? Do they leap tall buildings in a single bound? So call it as you see it...and tell them to do the same. But make sure you have a need for an SMO...a real SMO...and go get it. It could be the best business move you ever make.

9 HOW DO I KNOW IT'S THE RIGHT TIME FOR AN SMO?

Timing Is Everything

This question could have one, two, three **thousand** answers, but only a few apply to nearly everyone. Here's the back asswards way of determining your need for such an organization.

"You do not need an SMO if..."

1. You are content with your business as it exists in all respects.
2. You don't need new customers.
3. Expansion is not in the game plan.
4. Profitability is so high you're tickled pink.
5. You can't supply the demand for your products/services.
6. You're in danger of being labeled a monopoly if you get more business.
7. You just cashed in for the ostrich ranch in Texas, the golf course on Hilton Head, or the beach in Fiji.

Well, if you're a number seven candidate, tell us your secrets so we can all do that. Number seven people definitely do not need SMOs, so you can skip to the next chapter. In fact, you can skip the rest of this book with our compliments.

The primary thing to remember at all times is that number seven scenarios are most often found in the rapid eye movement (REM) part of your nightly dreams...for all intents and purposes they just don't exist. But keep hoping.

Analyzing responses 1 to 6

1. **The Completely Contented.** As far as believability is concerned, your batting average is zero. Nobody, Nobody, **NOBODY** is completely contented with their business to the point where they couldn't be made happier!
2. **Don't Need New Customers.** The only way this makes sense is if there aren't any more new customers or clients...meaning your raison d'etre might be just a bit suspect.

3. **No Expansion.** Unlike 1 and 2, this is possible. Changing technology actually makes this happen on a fairly regular basis. but this doesn't mean that you don't **WANT** to expand your business, but merely that you **CAN'T**...and even an SMO may not be able to help you do this...something they are apt to predict before they ever start working for you...like in your very first meeting.
4. **Tickled Pink with Profitability.** Lemonade is pink. Roses are pink. Elephants are pink when you've had a few too many. And if your profitability is so high you can't stand it, we think you're on intimate terms with pink elephants.
5. **Can't supply the demand.** Find a way to do it...or your competition will.
6. **Monopoly.** This means that you own Boardwalk, Park Place, the yellow color group, and a get out of jail free card. So expanding in another marketplace, arena, or country is still open to you.

So maybe you **do** need an SMO after all.

10 MEASURING YOUR NEED FOR AN SMO

First Things First

First of all, you have to accurately define what your business requirements are...make them consistent with a written business plan...for today and for tomorrow...then examine where marketing can help...then seek an SMO. So measure first...and be on target!

The following factors and considerations are merely a few that can aid greatly in determining your specific marketing needs.

Customer Nature

You may call them clients, buyers, or purchasing agents...end users, patients, or systems integrators...consumers, OEMs, dealers, or distributors...or *"the bane of my existence."* Whatever diverse names you term your customers, they all have one thing in common. They buy from you and therefore, they are the life's blood of your business. So take care — great care — to make sure you understand and appreciate your customers. Determine how well you know your customers. Know what they buy from you...and what they don't. Know why they buy from you...and why they don't. Learn why they buy in April and not October. Examine where your good sales leads and calls come from. Understand how your product/service is used in your customer's business. And know what you can do to aid your customer in doing better business.

Customer Volume

Is your customer volume ideal? Can you handle more business? How much more? 10%? 20%? 50%? Even more? Everyone knows that having all your eggs in one basket (or even two baskets) doesn't allow you to sleep nights if the basket represents your customer(s). If 80% of your business is one customer, that's a tenuous situation. For all the insomniacs reading this, make sure of the characteristic breakdown of your volume. Check it out!

Customer Loyalty

Three steps to success with this question are:
1. Ask yourself, *"Are my customers loyal?"*
2. Discard your answer.
3. Go ask your customers. Call them, speak to them, meet them, fax them. Find out what would happen if you violate one of the key components in your business relationship, e.g., delivery,

quality of product/service, etc. But don't violate it!

Strategic Needs

How well do you know the people who keep you in business? Have you measured their needs...not their whims, but their real, true, dyed-in-the-wool, unretractable needs? Do you know what they want? Do you know each and every service or product that will help them in their business or will advance their way of doing business? How important is timing? Inventory in stock? Quality of merchandise? Special services? Alternate solutions? Pricing? Quantity discounts? Know what they need from a strategic standpoint.

The Customer's Near Future

Do you know what their future needs are likely to be? Find out. Ask your customers. Research the market, the technologies, etc. But find out. FAST! And then gear yourself to be that indispensable resource that represents the future to them.

Top to Bottom

If the answer to the preceding thought is *"yes"* and you're a solo practitioner, you can rest comfortably assured that your organization isn't top heavy...that your company recognizes your clients' needs top to bottom. However, many businesses are somewhat larger. Are you 100% certain that **everyone** in your organization recognizes what your customers need and want? You'd better. It's essential. Does the company as a whole understand? Make sure!

Use Your Ears

Are you tuned in? Do you listen to your customers when they speak...or are you already formulating your next sales point when they're trying to communicate with you? Do you react to what they're saying? Do you react quickly enough? How do you know? Get the wax out and listen!

Proactivity

This isn't how many homeruns you hit but more like how you hit them. Let's assume your customer seeks information or data and asks you for it...and you deliver...on time. Is this a homerun? No. It's still a hit, a double perhaps because it was a reactive situation. Get the information to them **before** they ask for it. Be proactive. That's a home run. That's an SMO.

Supplier Loyalty

Everyone complains about customer loyalty, or rather the lack of it. How loyal are you to your customer? Do you go out of your way to ensure that all things are done to supply what he/she needs? Do it!

And that brings us to the concept of customer tailoring.

THE WAR FOR YOUR BUSINESS
A.K.A.
CUSTOMER VS. CUSTOMER
CUSTOMIZED VS. CUSTOMERIZATION
CUSTOM-TAILORED VS. CUSTOMER-TAILORED

War!

Your business begins and ends with your customer. No matter how you look at it, slice it, paint it, view it, consider it, examine it, alter it, etc., you're lying to yourself if you cannot appreciate this cardinal point. Your customer doesn't need you per se...he or she needs someone who can provide what you provide. Don't flatter yourself to the point of blindness. You're great, the best, blah, blah, blah, but you're not the only. And things can change. That's why war is a constant.

Back in the caveman days it was a pretty cushy situation to have the OOMBA Flint Franchise in Olduvai Gorge. Everyone needed flints for arrowheads, spearheads, hand axes, and other prehistoric cutlery. Sure, they could try cutting and shaping the flints themselves...and after the bloodletting was finished, there would be a major run on the OOMBA bandage franchise store. And then you downed a few at the waterhole and dragged yourself back to the OOMBA Flint Franchise and bargained for a workable unit or two. If you were lucky enough to be Mr. OOMBA, the end users came to you for flints. That is until some off-continent source began using chisels to mass produce your item...or worse, invented the machete or the bowie knife. You might retain some of your business, but the point is, your customer needs a service...not you...not necessarily.

If your customer is not at the center of your sales universe, ask yourself *"Why not?"* What else should be there? What else could be there? You might handcraft a wonderful six-piece set of strings for a violin...or make the best tasting cat food mix this side of Felineville, Arkansas...or print picture-perfect invisible ink, but your customers can't read invisible ink...Felix, Morris, Garfield, and friends may turn their finicky nostrils up at the cat food mix you think is so wonderful, and, by the way, violins only have four strings. So what are you doing? You've made yourself the center of your universe. No go. Make the customer your sun, your nucleus, your prime focus and then you're on the way to being **customer-tailored**.

Custom-tailoring vs. Customer-tailoring

(A) Custom-tailoring (or custom design) is a manufacturer-oriented, product-based concept. As good as it can be, it features five major drawbacks:

1. It does not **necessarily** establish a clear-cut concern for the client's business. It is generally limited to the client's product or service.

2. It delivers a sufficiently broad (almost nebulous) connotation that does not obviously consider support beyond the basic product, i.e., installation, delivery, software, QC, quality assurance, financing, etc.

3. By nature custom-tailoring is a reactive, not a proactive concept. The need has to be raised for the end to be created.

4. To potential clients, custom-tailoring something almost always connotes additional (often large) expenses for customization, e.g., alterations, special handling, etc.

5. Custom-tailoring provides no evidence or promise of supplier loyalty.

(B) Customer-tailoring is a need-oriented, solutions-based concept. It takes advantage of the concept of positioning.

1. The concern for the customer and the customer's overall business is of obvious preeminence.

2. It is of a focused nature to imply to the customer a strategic partnership that exceeds "widgets" and "frimstands"...it's not just limited to boxes sold and then the supplier disappears. Customer-tailoring implies the inclusion of elements that the customer wants, for the direct benefits of the customer.
3. The total solution concept of customer-tailoring can easily include all the factors to buy: service, quality assurance, financing, delivery, warranty, and any others, dependent on industry.
4. Customer-tailoring is proactive and promissory. It says, "We'll be there to service your business' needs. It's part of our service."
5. Customer-tailoring speaks of efficiency and does not readily deliver the thought of additional expenses...rather it says "We want your business, we have many resources and we'll deliver a solution that is the right one for your business."
6. By its very verbiage, it construes supplier loyalty. Just make sure you do it!

12 SUNNY-SIDE UP

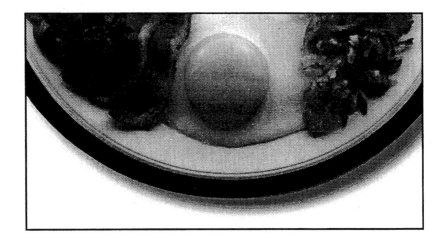

Putting All Your Eggs in One Basket: Selecting the Right SMO

First let me give you five arguments why you might not want to do this:

1. It's scary.
2. You're cutting out current trusted vendors.
3. You will not have total control.
4. Your empire won't be able to grow larger.
5. It's just not done!

Now, to refute 1 through 5.

Scariness

Of course it's scary. It's also terrifying, stressful, bewildering, anxiety-forming, nerve-wracking, and 20 or so more adjectives that we can all supply. Everything can be scary the first time. Remember riding your bike without training wheels for the first time? Can you recall your first day in a new school? Remember the first time you wound up with you-know-who in the backseat of a '66 Buick? So get over being scared about putting it all in one place. Get over being vulnerable. Get brave enough so you can at least contemplate the move. Weigh the pros and cons. Read this book! Then do it!

Excising Current Vendors

This can be a painful operation, both personally and business-wise. On the other hand, if you were receiving what you were paying for in the first place, you wouldn't be contemplating this move at all. If the vendor is your brother-in-law...well that's probably a mistake from the get-go. If the vendor is "absolutely super," ask yourself what makes them so good...their results...their salesmanship...their ability to attract bartenders in a crowded bistro...their handicap for 18 holes...and then analyze what you really are getting. If they're so wonderful with results...you can keep them, which may tend to undermine the broad scale results your SMO can offer...or you can introduce them to your selected SMO as a potential source. Put it in their hands. The SMO shouldn't feel threatened, and they won't regard it as a directive. Let them evaluate and decide.

Total Control

No you will not have total control. Yes, you will pass the reins, share the steering wheel, present the oars, surrender the compass, etc. Remember, total control is only a mindset for the insecure. Get real—ask yourself why you need total control. If it's your own company or practice, you can say *"Because I want to be the boss."* If you're a manager you can say *"Because I don't need more stress and my job is on the line."* Both responses are, as you well know, inadequate.

The reality of the situation is that you don't **need** total control so long as you have the final word. Let's call it **"ultimate control."** Remember, the SMO you're hiring is going to work **for you.** And answer to **you.** So keep ultimate control and pay attention to their plans. Critique them and above all, challenge them. Don't try to keep them off-balance or "hungry." You don't need to with an SMO. Design a systematic sign-off procedure that is realistic and doesn't stifle the SMO...just like you would for any other important arrangement. And use it. Remember, ultimate, not total control.

Empire Building

Empire building, as noted previously, works...if you're a paladin in Charlemagne's court, enamored of Alexander the Great, or permanently mind-stuck in Great Britain before World War I. It doesn't work in today's business world. It backfires more often than not. Empire building by nature is a recognizable device to push yourself up the ladder by utilizing/hiring personnel dedicated to promoting you first...and not necessarily the company. How long can that last? And don't think it will go unnoticed. What happens in a usual sequence is that the abilities of these so-called "loyalists" become secondary to their loyalty to you...so you're dealing with fawning sycophants, not dynamic supporters. If you really want to succeed, hire the best people you can find. Sure, someday they may be competition, but you found them and brought them on board to do the job in the first place. Get recognition for what you do, not for the size of your entourage.

It's Just Not Done

Times change. Before the 1960s it was unheard of for a man to have long hair. Once it was deemed impossible that the Soviet Union would crumble, that mankind could reach the moon, that living matter could be grown in a test tube, or that old baseball cards would be worth a small fortune. These were impossibilities...things that fall into the category of "can't be done" or "just not done." Well, putting all your eggs in one basket may be scary, require trust, sacrifice, hard work, good judgement, etc....but that's done all the time. Set yourself up with as tight criteria as you can imagine...and take the plunge...go get that SMO that's going to fit your plans and help you build your company's future. And do it now!

13 LEAVE NO STONE UNTURNED

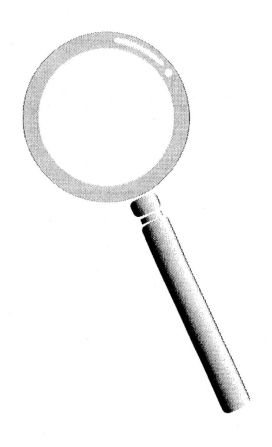

What should I consider in developing my list of criteria?

Consider **everything!** Then discard what you don't need. As a rule of thumb, the following certainly apply:

1. Who will actually service my account?

2. How do I know they will work hard for me?

3. Do they have to have experience in my field?

4. Can they understand the key aspects of my business?

5. Can they learn? Are they fast studies?

6. Will they be here when I need them?

7. Can they handle all aspects of my account effectively?

8. Are they stable as an organization?

9. How can I control costs and charges?

10. What if they've worked for my competition?

11. Aren't these steps a lot of trouble.?

12. How do I measure their effectiveness?

13. What if they can do it all?

14. What other factors can I include in my evaluation?

15. Do I need a contract with my SMO?

(1) Who?

It's a fair question. Once that key contact person is identified, reach out and get to know him or her. Ignore sloppy lipstick, baggy socks, or crooked ties. Look for the brightness in their eyes. Ferret out basic data like how long they've been involved with the SMO, and what industries they're versed in. Are they trained marketeers, or is their background writing, art, etc.? Find out their vital stats and dig until you're satisfied or you've annoyed them. Discover how they view their job relationship with you in terms of what their responsibilities are. Don't accept "whatever you want," "whatever you need," or "no problem." Get them to talk...and then tell them what you like and don't like. Measure them. Don't get stuck with a lemon.

When you have answers, try to make basic value judgements. You have to rely on this person. The word is **TRUST**! He/she is your contact, your direct link, your lifeline to the organization that you're paying for help. Explain in detail the way you'd like the business to be handled on a day-to-day basis. Listen to their comments, objections, or modifications. If they merely nod their heads, you're getting a yes-man or a yes-woman. If they protest and try to hem you in, you've got a control freak with tunnel vision. Both are inferior and dangerous. You need someone who can make meaningful suggestions or refinements to a procedure or project. Get someone who is a true team player and doesn't necessarily care where the idea or concept originated so long as it is definitely the best idea for you. You may view this as "Japan style" and it has worked marvelously for them...and it's the core of the SMO concept.

(2) Work hard for you?

You don't know this. No one is going to stand up and admit, *"I don't intend to hustle for you,"* or venture that," *I like to get in the office at 10:30 and get on the links by 2:00."*

Ask them directly, *"How do I know you're going to work hard for me?"* Their answer should warm the cockles of any SMO's heart. It should be... *"Our job is to learn and master your business to guide you strategically through the ferment of the unforeseen future...and you know how hard learning your business is...so you can be sure we — not just I — will be out there doing what is neces-sary. And as the old adage goes, we'll strive to work smarter, not necessarily harder."* Ahh, that should be music to your auditory canals.

(3) Experience in my field?

It certainly is a help if the SMO intimately knows your field. So define it for them as you see it from your vantage point. For exam-ple, let's assume you're a dental products distributor. Do you rule out the SMO if they have no dental background? No. Why? Because the dental part is technical and can be learned. In many cases it's easier than "unlearning." Then it's up to the SMO to convince you they can and will learn it...and state a time-frame and a game plan. But if they understand the distribution part, that's a huge plus. The SMO doesn't have to match up with everything you do...but there has to be a match **somewhere**. For them to learn the entire show...extant specifics, products, services, corporate philosophy and intentions, distribution channels, etc., means you have to be con-vinced as to their abilities to learn fast, under pressure. And the only way to do that, short of giving them your business, is to have them do a proposal. They may hate the idea (they shouldn't) but that's the way you want it. So do it! And they'll do it! If they balk, without a rationale, dump them fast.

(4) Can they understand?

If two meetings inundated with probing questions doesn't clearly reveal their abilities, you're on the wrong track and the train is com-ing full speed ahead. They should be asking pointed questions, off-the-wall questions, questions that defy logic, prompt demo and psy-cho graphic answers, assault sensitive business areas, require frank and honest answers, and make you both think. Make sure the SMO does this, or else they may be salespeople masquerading for capabil-ity.

(5) Can they learn?

Find out from their track record. Ask for a list of their clients (one that compares to the portfolio/slides/video samples they provide). Ask that each have a one- or two-line explanation of what the com-pany or organization does plus one or two lines on what the SMO did for them. Request their phone numbers and a key contact. Then do the dastardly unforgivable thing...call that key contact and find out all you can. *"Are they as fast on their feet as they seem? How fast did they learn your specifics? Did they have trouble with any aspects of your business and if so, which? Do they buy lunch? Are they timely with their proposals, drafts, ads, etc.? Do they ever miss deadlines?"* And don't just ask one client; ask as many as you need in order to form a strong opinion. Then, you ask for their list of former clients and find out why they are "former." After all this, if you're still unconvinced, it's time to hit the ejector button and jettison.

(6) Will they be here when I need them?

Of course not! More than likely you probably will be on a plane, at home, on the freeway, or at dinner when the urge strikes you. They don't have to be there holding your hand...but they have to be **available** at all times, having anticipated the need for their services. And with faxes, phones, computers, voice mail, and all of today's latest communications devices, you should be in close, if not constant, contact with them. Besides, if they're worth their fees, they'll be in contact with **YOU** when they need **you**. Proactivity! What a way to go.

(7) Can they handle my account effectively?

That's a toughie because it depends on what you require. And they will be the ones to inform you as to what you need to reach your goals. The quintessential SMO should be able to handle all strategic and tactical aspects of marketing including the implementation of:

advertising
article generation and placement
direct mail
general research
graphic design
media placement

media research
point-of-purpose
promotion
publicity/public relations
trade shows
etc.
etc.
etc.

They should be well versed in all these areas, not necessarily professionally educated, but with real-time, hands-on, twentieth century experience. Your pointman should have experience with all these areas. Probe deeply to find out the extent of his/her experience. If it's not enough, will this person hustle enough to do the right job? If it's still not enough and you're concerned about their ability to learn fast, ask for another point or contact person...or interview a few more SMOs.

(8) Are they stable?

Well, that's something that's relatively easy to measure. Ask them. Ask their clients. Ask their banks. Run a D&B. But find out first, **before** you hire them.

(9) How can I control costs and charges?

By writing down everything. Remember, an SMO isn't interested in a fly-by-night situation any more than you are. They're in it for the long-term. Their proposal should indicate specific costs. And where specifics are unrealistic, a budget or range should suffice. Have them commit all verbal promises and assurances to writing. In detail. With ranges, worst case scenarios, and no surprise definitions. For example, if ad film isn't included in ad production, you should know that up front. If they do six layouts for six data sheets and you specified three sheets, that's their problem. But if you asked for three variations of layouts for three different data sheets, nine designs total, expect to be charged. And pay for it. That's keeping up your part of the bargain, something the SMO will love you for...and will fuel them to work harder and smarter to maintain their end of the bargain.

(10) What if they've worked for my competition?

Well, bully for them. So what? This could run the gamut...good, bad, or indifferent. First things first. How did you learn that they represented your competition? Did they tell you up front or were you a good investigator and ferreted that out all by your lonesome? The former is professional. The latter means they might have wanted to hide it. If so, find out why.

Any SMO with even the least amount of integrity will be up front with you. If their intentions are to work with both you and your competition, handling all aspects of the two accounts, the concept of SMO could be compromised. To work with both accounts, but not handling all aspects of either, requires the insertion of a phrase... "non-disclosure," and it has to be in writing, in a nice legal contract. And then you have to have the confidence in their integrity that they will stand by it at all times. Otherwise, jettison time.

Physician, heal thyself. This opportunity can bring rare insights. Learn all the potentialities:

1. Make sure of the company's relationship to your competition.

2. Measure their industry knowledge by speaking to others who might know them, including consultants and media people, space salespeople, etc.

3. Ask them what they thought of your company while competing against you and what strategies they used. Don't accept glowing platitudes. Get the truth. You might think you already know the answers, but you could be very, very surprised.

Once that is done, analyze the results of their work to envision the situation. Ask yourself:

1. What were the short- and long-term results?
2. Did the campaign(s) or strategic marketing scenario(s) that they developed for your competition fully accomplish their goals? Make your own evaluation.
3. Did it exceed expectation? Fall short? Again, make your own evaluation.
4. How did that affect your company (long haul and short haul)?

Then evaluate them as you would any other company and make your decision. But don't let their previous business become a stigma.

(11) Aren't all these steps a lot of trouble to go to in choosing a vendor?

First of all, get the thought of **vendor**, in relation to an SMO, out of your head! Vendors sell hot dogs or peanuts or pretzels. An SMO markets your future. Second, who's to judge? Only you. Only you know how much a well-honed, customer-tailored, cost-effective marketing program could mean to your business or practice. Maybe you are happy with the amount of leads and the quality of leads you've received...and the exposure...and the image...and the potential for the coming year...and the stockholders love you. Maybe you're chugging along at 75% efficiency and that's good enough. (In fact, it might be a fine rating, if you're talking wood burning stoves.) And maybe maximizing your potential is no longer as important to you as it was 25 pages ago. Ask yourself: *Would I search as hard for an accountant? For a doctor to remove my gallbladder? Would I put in the time to find the right dentist, the right attorney?* Then why would you put in less time to help your business?

So you have to be the judge as to what you need, how much effort you should expend before you can hire even the best firm for your organization. Does the idea of maximum efficiency make sense? Does going as far as you can go make sense? How about eliminating the marketing ball and chain that may be holding you back? Once again, if you're one of those fortunate monopolies, you're safe...theoretically. But if you have competition, remember this: If you don't go after it, your competition, the other guys with the black hats and the red kerchiefs hiding half their faces, are going to pursue the new business stagecoach at your expense...and if they're smart fellas, they'll make sure that your posse never gets the chance to catch up. So hi ho Silver, head 'em off at the pass. Go get 'em! NOW!

Pursuing and choosing an SMO should not take a back seat if you have marketing needs. You don't have to be a superpower, a gigantic multinational company busy globalizing or downsizing or empowering...and in fact, you probably shouldn't be. You don't have to memorize the full tableau of today's nouveau high profile, marketech terminologies...you merely have to have a goal in mind, a definite goal with reasonable expectations. Then for all the western aficionados, Volunteer State, and Lone Star State readers, why not do as Davy Crockett said? *"First be sure you're right, then go ahead."*

And do it! No trouble should be too much. Fill the void. Close the gap. Fire the retro rockets. Be thorough. Do it, go to the trouble to find and hire an SMO, and reap the rewards.

(12) How do I measure their effectiveness?

Does getting 1,200 leads a month with your new program vs. 345 with your old program constitute effectiveness? Of course not! Certainly anyone agreeing that 1,200 leads a month vs. 345 is positive is an optimist who hasn't considered all the facts. Leads aren't the end in themselves. What constitutes effectiveness is the conformance to your established goals, those seemingly unattainable ends that you originally identified to your SMO...and you acknowledged by building a program to attain.

So identify your goals to yourself and your SMO. Create a hierarchy. Require them to produce a plan of attainment. Do everything you can to adhere to their program. If halfway through the program you decide it's too expensive to continue, then you've misguided yourself and your SMO. Measure success according to results...better recognition of the company name...products...line...reputation...better sales...better profitability. Make sure everyone is on the same sculling team or else everyone winds up...up the proverbial creek without a paddle.

(13) What if they can do it all?

What's your next question? Be more concerned about what if they can't do it all. Because then, they have to be ready, willing, and able to admit such, and have solutions available. If you're still worried about putting all your eggs in one basket, refer to the chapter titled "Sunny-Side Up." If you're still concerned, you're either considering an SMO imposter or you have problems trusting people in all facets of life. Find out what the SMO can do, and what they cannot do. And get on with it!

(14) What other factors should I consider?

Anything and everything.

(15) Do I need a contract?

Yes. Without a doubt. To be sure. Absolutely. Positively. 100%. Always.

14 How Do I Create an Effective Contract?

Not by Chance!

Turn on your PC, Macintosh, or mainframe...or your word processor or typewriter...or pick up your pen, pencil, or crayon...and start writing. Just make sure it's a letter to your attorney and **NOT** your own corruption of a real contract. Keep in mind one thing at all times...your contract is not akin to a protective tariff. It should not be set up so that you are in the driver's seat 100% of the time. Kill that urge. And don't let your attorney make the document completely one-sided no matter what he or she says. Let the attorney protect you but understand your business needs. And kill the urge to kill the attorney. Remember way back in the beginning of this book when we said an SMO is a different mindset? Well, we weren't kidding. An SMO-client relationship must be relatively equitable. After all, in essence you're strategically partnering, bringing a hired gun or specialist on board long-term to help grow your business. What you need like a hole in your head is a contract that can turn a good business arrangement into an adversarial situation ready to detonate and blow up so you lose all the hard-won victories. Don't get greedy, don't become paranoid, don't ever think you've put one over on your SMO like you put one over on your competition. They're on your side, and will be, until you hurl a monkey wrench into their well-oiled works.

Maximize your good will from the start.

Even so, a contract must be unilateral, so don't sell yourself short either. Concentrate on good business practices that you've learned in school or in the real world. The contract should be drawn up by **both** parties. Certainly one organization must take the lead and the actual burden of developing and executing the document. But for both sides several items must be included.

(1) Statement of interaction.

This can be as brief or as detailed as you wish it to be. Make sure to enumerate or provide detail on the specific items you are entrusting to the SMO. If, for example you are used to the traditional advertising agency, you'll be tempted to limit the responsibilities, simply because your experience tells you that while the agency might have performed admirably in some areas, their across-the-board performance may well have been too narrow, and therefore lacking. Your reluctance is understandable. Now lose it! Remember an SMO isn't an agency, it's a broad resource dedicated to you. So include the detail that accurately describes what you feel is correct...and listen to the SMO when (and if) they offer suggestions, alterations, and the like...and make sure your attorney OKs it all.

(2) Establish a reporting structure: who they'll report to, how, how often, etc.

Write it down so everyone is in agreement and there are no surprises. You'll get to hate surprises.

(3) Time Period!

A definite time period is necessary. Typically one year is the usual standard, but it could be one month if that's your operative frame. (We don't recommend that, however.) Whatever the frame is, specify it.

(4) Terms of billing and payment.

As in any business arrangement, these should be spelled out specifically. For example, the SMO will want to bill you upon completion of production items: ads, brochures, commercials, etc. Specify the terms in which you will pay these bills, e.g., 120 days from receipt (just kidding), Thirty days is most often used, but some businesses require C.O.D. or ten days, or 60 days, or payment up front. Whatever it is, set it down in writing...and then live by it! By paying late, you are violating the basic trust you've established with your SMO. Don't tell them they're a valuable resource, **show them**. Pay your bills as you said you would. Remember, the stronger they are, the more favorably disposed they are, the better service and end product you'll receive, above and beyond what you've contracted for. Don't weaken your SMO, strengthen them. And expect them to do the same.

(5) Escape Clause.

Speak to your attorney. Instruct him/her to have a clause that allows a graceful withdrawal or cessation after a reasonable getting-used-to period. No one should be saddled with a horse they don't want. Let the legal minds make reality out of your, and your SMO's, intentions.

(6) Retainer.

Let the screaming and crying commence! Insist on paying your SMO a retainer. Excuse me while I duck.

Why? It makes sense. A retainer, in the case of an SMO, is a fee that is regularly paid and keeps the SMO's thoughts on your **business** as opposed to your **account**. The fact is, the retainer is used to provide preferential service. It serves to spur the SMO to bravely go where no others have gone, to peek down the dark alley without wondering if there's anything worthwhile **for them** to benefit from. It obligates the SMO to go the extra mile all the time or at least in the instances that their talent and experience identify as having merit or potential.

Retainers don't have to cost an arm and a leg. A pinkie maybe. And if the SMO doesn't bring up the subject of a retainer, the client should. It is in both companies' best interests if a mutually acceptable retainer is developed. Just make sure it is accurately reflected in writing in your contract to protect both parties, and if you still have misgivings about this, perhaps you should keep looking. Think about it. Decide. Then do it. And put it in the contract.

15 ANY FINAL QUESTIONS?

Neither Fish Nor Fowl?

What other things are different with an SMO?

You are. Or should be. Don't ask for the impossible...growth and profitability are like guns and butter. They don't go well together for very long. Just ask LBJ. Don't expect an SMO to sell a poor product, service, or company. Don't tell them you're in it for the long haul when you really want to sell out and call it a career. Be up front. Be honest. Be realistic and make sure your SMO is realistic too. If you feel their plan is too expectant or too blue sky, tell them...if they persist, make them define their prediction...insist on a realistic approach that yields realistic results. If they hold that your expectations are too much too soon, don't close the door or hang up the phone, pick up where they left off. Find out why...analyze, weigh, and dissect their reasons. Are they right? Don't just tell them they're wrong or off base...if you can prove it, prove it. If not, do what they say. After all, they're the experts in this area.

Another "must" is to give your SMO the time they need. Make time. Call from your car phone or from your hotel, but call them or call them back. Answer their faxes and computer memos and voice mail or teleconferencing. Don't avoid them and don't avoid the issues....unless you want your business to work at less than maximum efficiency. Remember, they're your guys and gals. They're part of your investment in your business. Use them wisely.

Need more convincing? Do you have inside services? Would you agree that services as diverse as accounting, legal, and cleaning services are necessary to virtually all today's businesses. Why have them on staff when you can rent them? Why own a service with its overt and covert costs...with its tendency to Peter Principle, to defend itself first rather than be objective, and its ability to do three days work in five days...when you don't have to? Sure, if your needs for such services are so pervasive and constant that you need them every single day, not merely in your primary business, then you're in more than one business. In addition to your core business, you're in the business of upholding a hierarchy rather like Miss Liberty holding her torch. But for the vast majority, the cost-saving freedoms and potential benefits of using an SMO multiply as time passes. SMOs make sense! Learn it now! You heard it here first!

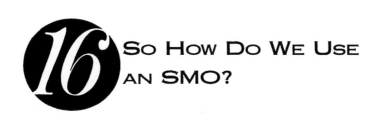

16 So How Do We Use an SMO?

How, Why, Who, When...?

"Well, that depends"...is the most ambivalent and dangerous phrase in the English language, and yet it applies. First you have to find an SMO. How? The way in which you uncover an SMO is relatively the same no matter your background, company size, product, or service. You open your eyes and ears and look for one! But the manner in which you **use** an SMO...depends on what kind of company, firm, or individual you are...and want to be.

The following two scenarios have been designed to represent cross sections of today's businesses. The names have been changed to protect the innocent. Actually both are fictitious companies; but these scenarios illustrate possibilities that could reflect reality as you know it. The first scenario demonstrates how an SMO might handle a new company launch, a manufacturing organization in a business-to-business environment. The second represents a hypothetical situation in which the SMO recommends a program for a cookie retailer to expand to a national scope. Browse as you will, and see if your thoughts are in any way similar to the SMO's recommendations.

The SMO and the Start-Up

Historical Perspective

Five young professionals have banded together, taken out second mortgages, borrowed from their respective Aunt Agathas, and put their as yet unwrinkled necks on the line for their new business venture. They feel they can market frimmels, because everyone knows what the world needs now is a better frimmel...and the kind that they will market is an industry-leading breakthrough...the *electronic frimmel!* Joe, Wanda, Phil, Steven, and Lupe met at Warren G. Harding Appreciation Night and the rest is hysterical...er...historical.

Where They Were At

Wanda was the V.P. at Felske's Frimmels, the industry's leading manufacturer. Chief Administrator there for 20 years, Wanda thought it was time to be paid for the aggravations she had to endure, and decided no one could pay her better than herself. The other four brought unique talents to the table, e.g., accounting and bookkeeping, sales, engineering, manufacturing, and marketing.

Market Conditions

There is a great need for a better frimmel in the USA, Europe, and the South Pacific...or so they all believe. Why? Frimmels are vital to the booming crimstan industry. Quality is of utmost import, and service (since frimmels could have significant downtime) ranks second. The sale does not end with product delivery, because frimmels consume large quantities of whatchamacallits. So selling frimmels is not the end of a relationship, it's the beginning.

Downsides

1. No one knows their company because it has just been formed.
2. No one knows their company's product since it is a first.
3. No one knows their company's position since they are new.
4. No one knows their company's reliability since they have no track record.
5. No one knows their company's customers since they have none.

Business Plan

Joe, Wanda, Phil, Steven, and Lupe, a.k.a., "The Gang of Five," have put together a rather exciting and yet financially realistic proposal. The business plan clearly indicates where they're at, where they can go to, where they are likely to go to, what it will cost, what the short-term needs are, what the long-term needs are, and what are the overall risks. In the proverbial nutshell, their business plan works...and it gets them the bank financing they need to launch the company and the product line. They're calling the new company *"Frimmels Are Us."* So now what?

Hunting Down the Correct Marketeer — or — Finding the Needle in the Haystack

They have it all covered, engineering through sale. What's next? They need advertising, they conclude. Or is it marketing that they need? Lupe thinks they'd better have a rationale, Steven calls it a strategy, and Joe wants to decide on tactics. All right, they finally conclude, maybe it isn't all covered. After interviewing an endless array of agencies, consultants, P.R. firms, strategic strategists, tactical tacticians, do-it-alls, see-it-alls, and know-it-alls, The Gang of Five scientifically pull numbers out of a hat and select the firm of **"Jones, Jones & Jones, Strategic Marketers."** (Well, we have to get them in the story fast!) And away we go.

17 ANALYZING THE STICKY WICKETS

Getting to first base

Working hand in hand with The Gang of Five, the Jones Boys ferreted out the information like hungry Klondike miners hitting the mother lode. Before The Gang of Five know it, Jones, Jones & Jones has them delving deeply into their own concept of realistic expectations, deadlines, agendas, quotas, market knowledge (and lack of), plans, etc. From this, the Jones Boys develop a remarkable scenario:

They do not rush out and design 11 four-color ads, six direct mail pieces, three new brochures, and a radio campaign. Not even a billboard. Instead, they first recommend a direct marketing channel... someone to sell the new frimmels...how about manufacturer's reps? Working with Steven who is a marketing person and Lupe, a salesperson, they help develop the rep network across the lower 48. These reps are experienced salespeople who will handle the frimmel line in addition to other existing (but hopefully not competing) lines. Since the reps already call on the buyers of frimmels you would think that frimmels, **wonderful electronic frimmels**, would be the reps' number one desire. You would think that they would instantly see the incredible value therein, would leap at the chance to sell these revolutionary items, making them so desirous of handling the line that things like motivation and credibility become a relatively simple matter; and of course, you would be entirely wrong.

Remember, first of all, that the reps were doing just fine **before** you happened on the scene. Sure some will push your product right away, but no success is guaranteed. After all, you're a new, unknown company with a potentially exciting, but unproven product. So now what?

Jones, Jones & Jones should know the answer. Realizing that no one is in business to watch the proliferation of electronic frimmels stack up in a warehouse (the one all five signed the loan for in blood), the SMO recommends a fair and just compensation package for the reps. This includes the right commission, certain sales incentives, and complete support. Joe, the financial type, objects and argues with Lupe the sales manager over the package. The SMO explains the difference between success and failure, and the package, somewhat modified, is instituted. (Can you imagine an agency or consultant refereeing this without the meter running?) So now The Gang of Five can just about count those frimmel sales rolling in already, right? Don't hold your breath.

Field representatives, and inside salespeople for that matter, can only go so far without the requisite sales items. Every industry is different, but let's assume the frimmel industry requires some of the following items: presentation pieces, samples, comparison data, instruction manuals, and data sheets. So where should *Frimmels Are Us* go? To an ad specialty house? To a printer? To a sales presentation company? Try your SMO. Jones, Jones & Jones know the market in advance, so that when the proper rep deal is structured and put into effect, there's nothing to stop these highly motivated, eager beaver salespeople. Right? Right.

Let's look at what's needed more closely.

Frimmel Samples

Frimmels Are Us needs to display the product. Buyers want to know that it is real. They want to touch it, drop it, spit on it, sit on it. Salespeople should always have samples and leave them behind with a prospect if feasible. If actual electronic frimmels are too large to transport or demo, miniaturized versions should be used. And buyers may think they're "really cute" in the bargain. More than one product has symbolically made its way on to a sales promotional keychain in this manner.

Sales Presentation System

Every rep needs one and may well appreciate such a system, particularly if it doesn't weigh too much. These can include portfolios of innumerable types, videos, slides, interactive media, flip charts, etc. It's something that effectively outlines, capsulizes, or cans the frimmel capabilities. You need to create and provide this. Get a specialist to do it right the first time...get your SMO to work on it.

Sales Literature

All too often the true buying decisions are not made by one person (particularly in Europe and Japan). This is especially true with capital equipment like frimmels. So what do you do? In larger buying institutions like hospitals, libraries, OEM manufacturers, multinationals, accounting and professional firms, organizations with multiple locations, buying may well be done by committee. Which means any snowstorm, heavy rain, mudslide, tidal wave, or comparable act of God is likely to keep the committee members from their appointed appointments...but not the *Frimmels Are Us* frimmel rep. Sales literature is designed to provide a guide for sales, and to pick up where the salesperson leaves off...by supplying the answers and solutions to the questions that those who missed the meeting will certainly have.

Comparison Data
Put in the competition. Compare them to *Frimmels Are Us* products feature by feature. Be honest.

Instruction Manuals
Do you think you can sell frimmels with one? Think again.

Jones, Jones & Jones, the SMO, will design, write, produce, and print the sales literature with the market in mind. Sales manager Lupe will be there to contribute, as will marketing manager Steven. In the case of electronic frimmels, the sales sheets will likely include copy areas such as description, application, features, benefits, specifications, options, rep imprint areas, logo, addresses, tag lines, etc. And they'll make sure a photo is used, not a drawing or rendering. Photos say *"It's here!"* Drawings and renderings say *"It's coming!"*

Wanda, the President of *Frimmels Are Us* (with a strong manufacturing background), listened to her SMO rather than the often conflicting needs of her reps, sales manager Lupe, financial man Joe, and Steven her marketing manager. The result? Sales literature perfect for its intended audience.

These may make a great deal of sense, but as Jones #1 pointed out, they're nothing, mere unconnected, unrelated vehicles without a unifying theme. *Frimmels Are Us*, he maintained, needed what all other companies also need: a program. So, "hold everything" was the order of the day.

The first thing any good SMO like Jones, Jones & Jones will do is to identify who, what, when, and where, and most importantly, why. Their proposal will include sheets that look a lot like those that follow and contain much information.

18 WALKING THE MARKETING TIGHTROPE

Identification Please!

As the old saying goes, the blindfolded dart thrower has the same chance of getting a bulls-eye as anyone, providing the contest takes place at night. Another way of saying it is even a broken clock has the right time twice a day. But why leave things to chance? It's too expensive. You're already on the marketing tightrope. Why not lessen the odds against you? To create a great program, start with the basics — identification. Jones, Jones & Jones put it all together.

IDENTIFYING OUR GEOGRAPHIES

Presently our promotional efforts are to be confined to the USA, Canada, and what used to be called Latin America in the days before political correctness. Europe and the Pacific Rim are targetable within 36 to 48 months.

Jones Jones & Jones
strategic marketers

IDENTIFYING OUR PRODUCTS AND SERVICES

Our product line currently consists of (3) electronic frimmels (#100, #200, #300) though primary sales emphasis is placed on #100. Service and support will be treated as "product" in this campaign from the standpoint that they play a large role in the decision to purchase a frimmel, particularly in the crimstan and doleberk market sectors.

IDENTIFYING OUR TARGET AUDIENCES

The target audiences for our extant product line of electronic frimmels are varied and distinct within the confines of several industries. This centers around the crimstan industry, but large-scale applications also exist in doleberks, jackmoeys, neuronostalgia, and the emerging gigahumana industry. For our Frimmel 100 the key target audience for penetration is largely within the crimstan area. For our Frimmel 200, the prime target is doleberks. For our Frimmel 300, the key target audience for penetration is any market regardless of size which is currently performing frimmel testing of any type. Currently we see the target market for *Frimmels Are Us'* current line to consist of:

Administrative Administrators

Capital Equipment Decision Makers

Clinical Clinicians

Directors

Key Purchasing Personnel

Operations Managers

Purchasing Agents and Buyers

Supervisors

Systems Engineers

Systems Managers

Technical Technologists

Virtually anyone with purchasing influence

Jones Jones & Jones
strategic marketers

IDENTIFYING THE COMPETITION

Our competition consists of several well-known, well-entrenched, well-respected firms. In the crimstan and doleberk sectors they include: Felske's Frimmels, Crimstan Frimmels, ABC Frimmels, and other equally formidable companies. Neuronostalgia is largely owned by Felske's, with a market share of 62%. Gigahumana, a new applications area, is wide open.

By viewing these four identity sheets, Steven, the marketing manager should be tickled pink, or at least fuschia. This should jibe precisely with the descriptions in the General Business Plan. If they do not, it's likely that the SMO research is superior or more recent. So the SMO would then bring Wanda and the rest of The Gang of Five, up to date on what's what.

19 PROVIDING FRIMMELS ARE US WITH REALISTIC PROGRAM GOALS

Vs.

Mass Market Goals

The SMO then worked its way into the specific goals they wished to achieve. The following sheets are ideal types of what aspects need review. There are three categories (A, B, and C) since proper basic positioning as handled by an SMO must not be limited and must address the company, the products, and the sales channels.

Jones Jones & Jones
strategic marketers

A. *Frimmels Are Us:* The Organization

The promotional campaign contained herein is designed to identify, target, penetrate, and positively influence the major audiences for *Frimmels Are Us,* the company, and its products/services. In one sense, it is a true positioning statement. Our campaign is comprehensive in that it creates, establishes, identifies, and details vital messages...specifies proven reach vehicles...and provides a means of fulfillment. In this sense it is a valid sales campaign. Either way it is a classic double-decked campaign in that we are positioning and promoting both product(s) and company image. For *Frimmels Are Us* our program goals are to establish the image of the organization as:

1) A quality supplier of quality products and services.
2) A stable organization targeted for the long haul.
3) Innovative in our product approach and mix.
4) Innovative in our means of doing business.
5) A company concerned about its people, its customers, its suppliers.
6) A company that is a recognizable leader in technology and product development.
7) Both dependable and reliable above the norm of the industry.
8) A dynamic company that is changing in a very positive, planned manner.
9) A company that must be considered when contemplating a purchase.

Jones Jones & Jones
strategic marketers

B. *Frimmels Are Us* Products

By implementation of this campaign we will:

1) Achieve market launch, recognition, retention, and appreciation of the *Frimmels Are Us* product line.

2) Detail, delineate, and establish *Frimmels Are Us* products, in particular Frimmels 100, 200, and 300.

3) Generate legitimate inquiries and attract new, qualified sales leads.

4) Establish the fact that our customer commitments are long-term, and that we have been and intend to be active on a permanent and successful basis.

5) Create a favorable environment for the introduction of forthcoming new/improved *Frimmels Are Us* products and services.

6) Create a sense of anticipation that we will have new products.

7) Provide a key thematic tie-in for our annual trade show efforts.

C. *Frimmels Are Us* Service and Support

By implementation of this campaign we will:

1) Establish that we are extremely concerned with quality of product and quality of service.

2) Establish appreciation of our position re: custom and multiyear contracts, guaranteed uptime, guaranteed response time, etc.

3) Reveal our progress in terms of service and relate that we will not rest on our laurels or on anyone else's laurels.

4) Underscore the stagnant state of other competitive services.

5) Establish that we have an excellent record of service and product support.

6) Provide a key opportunity to tie into our annual trade show schedule.

Jones Jones & Jones
strategic marketers

D. *Frimmels Are Us* Selling Side Goals

By implementation of this campaign we will:

1) Create a definitive "*Frimmels Are Us* line" (theme) for our sales force to follow.

2) Establish a positive corporate image to enhance recognition.

3) Clearly define and provide necessary hands-on leadership, positioning, and strategy for our salespeople to utilize.

4) Create the most fertile market environment for field and internal salespeople to sell in.

5) Recommend, produce, and provide all necessary internal and external sales items for our sales force to utilize.

6) Help *Frimmels Are Us* better coordinate the release of our information with the sales force in mind, keeping the sales force educated as to product merits, advantages, selling scenarios, as well as promotional time scheduling.

7) Utilize established promotional and positioning themes to help sales personnel reduce the time to close a sale.

8) Expand the campaign theme to help salespeople with pull-through at major shows.

9) Reinforce and substantiate all direction provided by all *Frimmels Are Us* programs, spiffs, promotions, etc.

10) Provide everything needed so that sales force can pass the time-honored McGraw-Hill "Field Test."
   - I don't know who you are.
   - I don't know your company.
   - I don't know your company's product.
   - I don't know what your company stands for.
   - I don't know your company's customers.
   - I don't know your company's reputation.
   - Now — what was it you wanted to sell me?

Once again, the goals as outlined by Jones, Jones & Jones, the SMO, should coordinate perfectly with the original plans and goals. Wanda and company should be getting excited since the prerequisites for selling hundreds of thousands of electronic frimmels are right on the moola.

20 POSITIONING THE COMPANY

Where From? Where To?

Explaining Strategic Positioning

This, of course, takes a few days to sink in. However, no one exposed to strategic positioning for the first time can admit that fact, since this is deemed common knowledge, common sense, good business sense, etc. That's a load of buffalo chips since positioning can be Pavlovian, but depends on the source. So it can be many things. Positioning is a relatively simple and dynamic concept. **Strategic positioning works!** When applied to product sales development, we define strategic positioning as the process of:

Firmly establishing a product's benefits in the perception of the target audience...so when exposed to the need for the benefit, the target automatically recalls the product.

After all, success is not dependent on what **you** think of your product or service or company...**success is dependent on what your target audience thinks of your product or service or company.**

The value of positioning is easily understood: **short- and long-term target audience retention** of offerings...products, company, support, and our *raison d'etre*. Positioning is a communication channel that will be harvested continually over time in terms of sales. A carefully honed and maintained position will sell *Frimmels Are Us* and *Frimmels Are Us* products for years to come.

How Jones, Jones & Jones used Strategic Positioning with Frimmels Are Us

The SMO explained to Wanda, Joe, Phil, Steven, and Lupe the incredible reach of successful electronic frimmel positioning. They pointed out that full utilization began when initial market penetration was completed, and both *Frimmels Are Us* and *Frimmels Are Us* products were well positioned within the selected marketplaces. Jones, Jones & Jones utilized this newly established position to lend instant credibility to new products and capabilities, and to create faster acceptance and measurable sales.

PRODUCT POSITIONING

The FR-100, FR-200 and the FR-300 are existing products in our line. Advantages offered are broken down in no particular order of importance:

100	•Cost-effective. No waste
100	•No operator interaction: runs by itself
100, 200	•Immediate STAT override achieved in three seconds or less
All	•24 hour standby always ready, no warm up
100	•Excellent throughput: really puts the "crim" in crimstan
All	•Convenience
200	•Excellent conductivity
100	•"Max efficiency" features: saves time, money
300, 200	•Minimized consumption and associated costs
300, 200	•Fast delivery: available from stock
All	•Low maintenance: service contracts available
All	•Guaranteed accuracy: never misses a "crim" or "stan"
300, 200	•Low consumables
300, 100	•Easily installed

Naturally, the values detailed above will be explained/reflected in the approaches to the end users.

Jones Jones & Jones
strategic marketers

PRODUCT POSITIONING: Service and Support

The days when service/support were relegated to an inferior role are long over. With the state of the economy, anxiety over the Federal government's role, and the regulation proposed by CLIA, SEC, OSHA, FCC, FDA, and dozens of other similar acronyms, service and support must be considered to be a major sales factor, i.e., "a product." Our efforts are concentrated on establishing the following benefits in the minds of our target audiences. These are general and are in no way intended to be actual copy. Rather they are benefit points. The benefits include:

- *Frimmels Are Us* proactivity: we don't wait, we just do it.
- Availability and flexibility of custom and multiyear contracts: saves you money.
- Extent of guaranteed pricing for term of contract.
- Status of *Frimmels Are Us* guaranteed response time.
- *Frimmels Are Us* guaranteed uptime.

 # GETTING SPECIFIC

How the SMO's recommendations navigated the icy, cold waters of the product sales seas.

Avoiding Scylla (too little promotion, too late) and Charybdis (a fun, clever, award-winning campaign that doesn't sell electronic frimmels or electronic frimmel makers) is the first thing the SMO put forth in their strategic odyssey. Like all sensible SMOs, Jones, Jones & Jones found it vital to expose the basic elements of what the campaign was to consist of...and why they were recommended.

Jones Jones & Jones
strategic marketer

TACTICAL ELEMENTS FOR *FRIMMELS ARE US:*

Tactical elements are those items that will carry the messages to our targets. Our campaign includes:

1) True thematic campaign space advertisements — phases one and two.
2) Print media schedule and placement.
3) Key collateral offerings to target audiences.
4) Corporate mission statement for external distribution.
5) Support and service statement of fact.
6) Salesperson's guide to the new campaign.
7) Sales presentation materials.
8) Sales promotional items.
9) Publicity.
10) Trade show background and overview.

Why all these elements? What is a phase campaign? Why a virtual training guide to our experienced sales force? Why a mission statement? Why? Why indeed...these are all viable questions. Read on and ye shall receive the answers.

Jones Jones & Jones
strategic marketers

TACTICAL ELEMENT ONE: THE MEDIA CAMPAIGN

After careful consideration, it is obvious that potential customers for our products can (and will) ask the following:

a) "Why should I stick my neck out for recommending or buying a product/company that I don't know...is "new"...has no track record...doesn't have a recognized reputation for service and support, or financing innovation...and hasn't convinced me that it can be my resource, my provider, my supporter, my loyal dependable Friday, Watson, Robin, Chingachgook, etc.?"

Good question. This is not an unrealistic attitude for potential buyers to have at this time...and this can severely hamstring a salesperson's efforts. Our campaign will address and overcome this. What we must achieve is the status to be considered in any buyer's decision to purchase a frimmel. The campaign gets right to the heart of the matter...we'll not blow smoke, use mirrors, create a diversion, etc..., but forge ahead putting our considerable resources forth on a merit basis. Rather than hide, we expose...rather than create excuses, we present facts...rather than sidestep, we attack.

CAMPAIGN STRATEGY: SEGMENT ONE

Ad #1 Head: Our Frimmels won't make you wait...
Ad #1 Subhead: but they will make your day.
Ad #1 Tag: Remember. *Frimmels Are Us.*

Ad #2 Head: No Frimmel frims like the F-300...
Ad #2 Subhead: with electrifying results.
Ad #2 Tag: Remember. *Frimmels Are Us.*

Ad #3 Head: There's a lot behind our Frimmels...
Ad #3 Subhead: and it's all in writing.
Ad #3 Tag: Remember. *Frimmels Are Us.*

Ad #4 Head: The best service response time guarantee you'll never use.
Ad #4 Tag: Remember. *Frimmels Are Us.*

Jones Jones & Jones
strategic marketers

CAMPAIGN STRATEGY: SEGMENT TWO

After the successful implantation of the campaign in segment one, segment two will differ as follows:

We will proceed to full standard page ads (also called junior pages in tab publications) based on topics (Frimmel 100, Frimmel 200, Frimmel 300, service and support, *Frimmels Are Us*, the organization). The reasons are grounded in hard facts: we need real estate and frequency to discuss all our points in detail...and our budget is not unlimited.

(1) Head: If it works great and works great and works great...
Subhead: it's FR-300.
Tag: Remember. *Frimmels Are Us.*

(2) Head: Purchasing your first electronic Frimmel?
Subhead: Why not settle for more for less?
Tag: Remember. *Frimmels Are Us.*

(3) Head: When crimming and stanning are headaches...
Subhead: we offer relief.
Tag: Remember. *Frimmels Are Us.*

Jones Jones & Jones
strategic marketers

TACTICAL ELEMENT TWO: EXPANDED MEDIA CAMPAIGN

As noted, we must expand our media placement schedule in the launch stage of our campaign. However, we will reduce space size in the second phase or stage, following our primary trade show and other major shows. (See media schedule.) In addition, we have negotiated favorable pricing regarding media, including a waiver of special positioning charges, a rollback to last year's rates and reduced rates in various publications.

TACTICAL ELEMENT THREE: KEY COLLATERAL PROMOTIONS

We believe it is absolutely vital to establish *Frimmels Are Us*...not merely as a provider...but also as an authority! This is the best position to sell from and arms our reps properly. The timing is perfect...since our audience is essentially "unfamiliar" with us. We cannot write the "bible"...there's not enough time...so we'll create three of them! These will consist of quick overviews, providing thoughtful incisive guidance, glossaries, (allegedly) unbiased information. They will answer "why" and provide "how-to" answers and solutions. They're actually quick guides or expanded checklists that our potential customers will want. Why? Because they are:

1) directed to help them with topics they value highly.
2) designed to help our target audience professionally.
3) available free of charge.

Essential to the success of this campaign is the offering of unbiased, no frills, how-to guidebooks. Copy will be straightforward and professional. Content will be generated and finalized via joint effort. Typically eight to 12 pages, digest sized, will be offered item for item with each fractional page ad, and all three with the full tab page summation ad. The guidebooks are:

(A) Head: PURCHASING
    Subhead: Your electronic frimmel. A How-To-Guide.

(B) Head: SELECTING
    Subhead: The best provider for your frimmel needs...A How-To-Guide.

(C) Head: SUPPORTING
    Subhead: Your electronic frimmel...A How-To-Guide.

Jones Jones & Jones
strategic marketers

THE BENEFITS TO *FRIMMELS ARE US*

1) **Recognition:** Each and every time a reader refers to these "pocket guides," they're acknowledging *Frimmels Are Us* as an expert...which is part and parcel of what we're trying to achieve in our campaign.

2) **Appreciation:** These items are offered free of charge by phone, fax, reader service, etc. This brings *Frimmels Are Us* into mind with a positive thought.

3) **Leads and Mailing Lists:** *Frimmels Are Us* has options of how to follow up and has successfully opened communication channels.

4) **Rep Recognition:** Reps can personally hand out a truly useful "save" piece, a "non-sales" item.

5) **Inexpensive:** Other than details and writing composition, these are very fast and inexpensive to produce and print.

6) **Unbiased:** However, positive, weighted references to *Frimmels Are Us* can be included.

7) **Availability:** We urge these to be made available on diskettes.

Jones Jones & Jones
strategic marketers

TACTICAL ELEMENT FOUR: MISSION STATEMENT

This would be a "corporate" item, one that "establishes policy in a non-policy format." A brief 8 1/2" x 11" or 11" x 17" sheet, this is intended for external distribution. It will explain **how** we are in business, **why** we are in business, and **whom** we are in business to support. It can be as extensive as we like or as brief as we like; it should be used by reps on sales calls, in binders with all forms, presentations, etc. It should be used in other ways also, from informing the media, to informing Wall Street, the competition, and foreign markets.

Jones Jones & Jones
strategic marketers

TACTICAL ELEMENT FIVE: SUPPORT/SERVICE STATEMENT

Expanding on the theme established in the advertising campaign, this service brochure will be a simple 8 1/2" x 11" or 11" x 17" sheet. Its purpose is to provide an informational overview of our full capabilities, custom and multiyear contracts, guaranteed uptime, guaranteed response time, etc., in detail. It is our "position statement" for service.

Jones Jones & Jones
strategic marketers

TACTICAL ELEMENT SIX: SALESPERSON'S GUIDE

Our manufacturer's reps and internal salespeople are the essential vanguard in our promotion and we must have excellent communication with them providing campaign rationale and strategy long before the campaign breaks. This guide is an instructional summary piece that will fit the bill. This need not be a fancy or expensive piece; the point is to be informative, easy to read, and easy to absorb. This is for **the salesperson only**...not for customers, users, operators, etc. "Why?" you might ask...because we need to have the sales force behind us and behind the program at all times...following the thematic approach established by Marketing...well before potential customers see our campaign (sales manager Lupe loves the idea). This is the forum to explain why...how...who...what...and where...to the people who need to know what to expect and what to say...to the people who will eventually buy our products, services, or company. It can, for all intents and purposes, be offset printed...**it's the content that is vital**...to unify our sales effort in every detail. The piece will not tell the reps how to sell...they already know that...but it will direct their attention to various parts of the campaign.

Jones Jones & Jones
strategic marketers

TACTICAL ELEMENT SEVEN: SALES PRESENTATION MATERIALS

The need for an interesting, cohesive, in-person sales presentation is paramount. Interactive multimedia is exciting and "au courant," but too expensive for a new company like *Frimmels Are Us*. Timing and cost put it out of the question at this time. Other candidates are a video, a slide presentation, flip charts, campaign reprints, etc. By surveying the market (in conjunction with marketing manager Steven) we discover that virtually all our potential audiences have VCRs at their offices...a VCR promotional sales tape can be quite effective. Jones, Jones & Jones' recommendation is to produce a seven-to-ten-minute video (not too long to have them fall asleep, not too short to omit anything). Budget-wise a video can cost from a few thousand to many thousands of dollars. A budget is enclosed. Jones, Jones & Jones will create the script and scenario, then hire and supervise a video production house to professionally produce the sales tape. All is included in the budget.

Jones Jones & Jones
strategic marketers

TACTICAL ELEMENT EIGHT: SALES PROMOTIONAL ITEMS

We recommend supplying reps with promotional items that their accounts and potential customers will want. They should be tied directly to our media campaign theme.

Jones, Jones & Jones chose tee shirts. Why do we suggest an item such as a tee shirt? Isn't this too...pedestrian? Does this lack vision? No and no. Everyone wants one, wears one, uses one...which puts our sales message in front of a large audience...making it a living advertisement. Also, the people who actually run the electronic frimmels often dress casually — and a classic, well-made, well-designed shirt will put our name in front of them on a regular basis. We've budgeted for such an item. However, there are dozens of additional items that could be used as selling tools at rep visits from wristbands, magnets, pens, and calendars, to mugs, funnels, magnifying glasses, and labware. The vital part is to use them at sales calls, to influence, to remind, and to reward. Promotional items work and we've included a budget for such.

Jones Jones & Jones
strategic marketers

TACTICAL ELEMENT NINE: PUBLICITY

Perhaps the most cost effective and vital link in the marketing chain, publicity is a vital vehicle to use fully and often. Currently we have the following releases scheduled:

News Release	Status
Frimmels Are Us Formed	mail 12/1
Wanda Appointed President	mail 12/6
FR-100	mail 1/14
FR-200	mail 1/23
FR-300	mail 1/28
Frimmels Are Us Adds Rep in:	
•Northeast	mail 2/18
•Southeast	mail 2/25
•Midwest	mail 3/04
•Rocky Mountain Area	mail 3/11
•California	mail 3/18
•Northwest	mail 3/25
•Southwest	mail 4/01
•Puerto Rico	mail 5/08
•Vancouver, Canada	mail 5/15
•Quebec, Canada	mail 5/22
•Mexico City	mail 5/29
•Buenos Aires	mail 7/15
•Rio de Janeiro	mail 7/22
Frimmels Are Us to Attend Crimstan World	mail 3/10
Phil to host Seminar at Crimstan World	mail 3/17
Frimmel Brochure Available	mail 4/08
Frimmels Are Us Opens New Factory	mail 8/10
FR-100 Software Update	mail 8/17

Our recommendation here is to maintain an ongoing program: produce and disseminate as much viable publicity as possible in the form of news releases, articles, feature listings, etc. This requires a close relationship, so at regular meetings, we will bring up the topics, needs, deadlines, etc., with Steven, our single point of contact.

Regarding Trade Shows

"Crimstan World" is the industry's largest, most respected, and most attended trade show. Everyone in the crimstan industry will be there, plus a large percentage of attendees will be buyers from the doleberks, neuronostalgia, and the jackmoey/gigahumana segments. All the competitors will have display exhibits there, including industry leader Felske's Frimmels. Wanda, a former Felske V.P., wants to "bury" Felske at the show. Sales manager Lupe needs to demonstrate "aggressive power." Marketing manager Steven wishes to "identify every potential lead in the show." Phil the engineering director wants to see what's new and will host a seminar on what's not. Even Joe the financial expert recognizes the opportunity and is ready to allocate a b-i-g budget. And Jones, Jones & Jones, the SMO, has a big stake and something to prove. So the company should be allocating a huge budget to thoroughly saturate their audience, right? Guess again.

As an SMO, Jones, Jones & Jones will not succumb to the dreaded agency-PR mumbo jumbo. Their concern isn't merely to make a big splash —they have to be concerned that they spend appropriately —in other words:

- enough to make the *Frimmels Are Us* first appearance a success.
- enough to show the reps that *Frimmels Are Us* is supporting them in a wise manner.
- not too much so that their extant promotional plan is compromised.
- not too much so that they could not pull from a contingency fund to take advantage of targets of special opportunity that may pop up unexpectedly.
- enough so that success can have pre-determined goals, tempered by show realities.

Jones, Jones & Jones is an experienced SMO. They know new companies can, and often do, spend foolishly and unnecessarily in preparing for these situations. They need everyone's involvement. Certainly Wanda is personally involved, but not strategically. And Lupe and Steven may be overwrought. Instead of yielding to pressure, the SMO refuses to squander their budget on a 150′ x 150′ exhibit area. Instead, they recommend a 20′ x 20′ booth space and explain why.

Jones Jones & Jones
strategic marketers

TACTICAL ELEMENT TEN: TRADE SHOWS

1) As a new company, why start off huge and possibly have to downsize for next year's show? That's potentially projecting a negative.

2) As a new company with much advance publicity, potential buyers will stop in to "discover" *Frimmels Are Us*. After all, these are professional buyers.

3) Our in-place advertising and advance public relations will have announced our show attendance.

4) Many reps who know the buyers will be attending and will file prospects by the booth.

5) The Gang of Five, in particular industry leader Wanda, will receive attention from their industry acquaintances.

6) The SMO has arranged an article in *Frimmels Today* magazine breaking in the pre-show issue, stimulating interest that will carry over to the show.

7) The SMO has booked print advertising space in the daily show issues of *"The Journal of Crimming and Stanning"* with directories ("see us at booth #4444").

8) The SMO has booked a PR press session for the morning of the second day of the show.

9) A special seminar has been arranged by the SMO for the first night re: *"Launching a New Electronic Frimmel Company."* Wanda and Joe are scheduled to speak.

10) The SMO has designed and built, in conjunction with an exhibit builder, an attractive, highly functional trade show display.

11) We have put together a contest with prizes for attendees.

12) The SMO has the company listed and profiled in the show guide.

Jones, Jones & Jones' SMO-oriented plan will accommodate everyone's trade show concerns. Moreover it demonstrates the depth of thinking and ability to create and implement that an SMO simply has to possess. After presenting their points, Jones, Jones & Jones returned to the tactical approach.

They coordinated the new thematic approach from *Frimmels Are Us* advertising with the new trade show booth. *Frimmels Are Us* will be able to capitalize graphically in every way...establishing the questions and answers, and displaying models 100, 200, and 300 at every station or stanchion. The SMO recommended inclusion of a "service center" as well as a multi-media center. A shortened, "looped" version of the video was expected to be a winner and attention-getter. The campaign graphics lent themselves to large blow ups, particularly when converted to translights ("see-throughs") to be the fronting for design-in light boxes, projections, multi-media, etc. In any event, *Frimmels Are Us* will be able to feature campaign slogans, art, photos, etc., at the booth to tie in with current advertising and promotions, well-educated and well-versed sales reps, etc....to create as comprehensive a package as can be established.

22 CREATING A REALISTIC BUDGET

Creating the realistic budget: How the SMO came through.

It is everyone's least favorite word. It is also everyone's biggest excuse. Some call it a "necessary evil," others omit "necessary." However, regardless of your viewpoint or perspective, a budget is necessary in business. Of course, a budget is only as good as the parameters that go into it, so everything needs to be evaluated, weighed, considered, and re-considered. Flexible budgets, those that stretch and shrink with real world applications, make the most sense. So put together a budget based on true expectations. Make it flexible. And stick to it! The SMO did precisely that for *Frimmels Are Us.*

Jones, Jones & Jones, Strategic Marketers, 1234 Main Street
Carbuncle, IA 45678 • Tel: (444) 444-4444 • Fax: (444) 444-4445

FRIMMELS ARE US

MEDIA SCHEDULE — JANUARY - DECEMBER

PUBLICATION	JAN	FEB	MAR	APR	MAY	JUN	JUL	AUG	SEP	OCT	NOV	DEC
Frimmels Today 6X $3,710		1		2	3 Preshow	**			4	5	6	
Frimmels Today Buyers' Guide 1X $3,760									1			
Neuronostalgia Lit. Showcase 2X $2,010										1	2	
Dolebecks Post Cards 3X $2,280	1					2						3
Jml of Crimming & Stanning 6X $2,600	1		2		3		4		5		6	
Jackmoey World 6X $2,245		1		2		3		4		5		6
Jml of C & S Directories 3X $2,000			1			2			3			

**Crimstan World Show

TOTAL EXPENDITURE = $71,950.00

117

Jones Jones & Jones
strategic marketers

BUDGETS

ELEMENT I: CAMPAIGN AD PRODUCTION

Segment One
(1) Full tab page, 4C ad	$ 12,500.00
(3) Junior page, 4C ads	$ 21,500.00
(3) 1/2 Tab variations of Junior page, 4C ads	$ 7,500.00
(1) Junior page, 4C ad variation	$ 2,500.00
TOTAL	**$ 44,000.00**

Segment Two
(3) Junior page, 4C ads	$ 12,500.00
(3) 1/2 Tab variations of Junior page, 4C ads	$ 7,500.00
(1) Junior page, 4c ad variation	$ 2,500.00
TOTAL	**$ 22,500.00**

ELEMENT II: MEDIA

Frimmels Today (6) Full page 4C ads @ $3,710 =	$ 22,260.00
Frimmels Today Buyers' Guide (1) Full page 4C ad @ $3,760 =	$ 3,760.00
Neuronostalgia Lit. Showcase (2) Full page 4C ads @ $2,010 =	$ 4,020.00
Doleberks Postcards (3) Cards B/W @ $2,280 =	$ 6,840.00
Journal of Crimming & Stanning (6) Full page 4C ads @ $2,600 =	$ 15,600.00
Jackmoey World (6) Full page 4C ads @ $2,245 =	$ 13,470.00
Journal of Crimming & Stanning Directories (3) Full page 4C ads $2,000=	$ 6,000.00
TOTAL MEDIA	**$ 71,950.00**

Jones Jones & Jones
strategic marketers

ELEMENT III: KEY COLLATERAL

Complete production of (3) 8- or 12-page "how-to" guides:
"Purchasing;" "Selecting;" "Supporting" @ $3,000 = $ 9,000.00
Printing of 1,000 pieces each of the
    above @ $1,500 = $ 4,500.00
                  TOTAL   **$ 13,500.00**

ELEMENT IV: CORPORATE MISSION STATEMENT

Complete production of (1) 8 1/2" x 11" or 11" x 17"
    mission statement $ 1,500.00
Printing of 1,000 pieces of above $ 1,250.00
                  TOTAL   **$ 2,750.00**

ELEMENT V: SUPPORT/SERVICE STATEMENT

Complete production of (1) 8 1/2" x 11" or 11" x 17"
    piece $ 1,750.00
Printing of 1,000 pieces of above $ 1,500.00
                  TOTAL   **$ 3,250.00**

ELEMENT VI: SALESPERSON'S GUIDE

Complete production $ 2,000.00
Printing of 1,000 pieces of above $ 1,500.00
                  TOTAL   **$ 3,500.00**

Jones Jones & Jones
strategic marketers

ELEMENT VII: SALES PRESENTATION MATERIALS
Production of (1) sales video @ $25,000 =
Duplicating (1) sales video 500 @ $12.00 =

	$ 25,000.00
TOTAL	$ 6,000.00
	$ 31,000.00

ELEMENT VIII: SALES PROMOTIONAL ITEMS
A) 1,000 4C Tee Shirts @ $5.50 =
B) Original Art
C) Contingency Budget

	$ 5,500.00
	$ 2,000.00
TOTAL	$ 5,000.00
	$ 12,500.00

ELEMENT IX: PUBLICITY
Budget

$ 15,000.00

ELEMENT X: TRADE SHOW BOOTH
A) Design and Fabrication
B) Graphics

	$ 35,000.00
TOTAL	$ 15,000.00
	$50,000.00

ADDITIONAL ITEMS
Sales Sheets, 3 @ $4,000 =
Printing of Sales Sheets, 1,000 pcs. =
Instruction Manual Production =
Printing of Instruction Manual, 1,000 pcs. =

	$ 12,000.00
	$ 7,500.00
	$ 5,000.00
TOTAL	$ 2,250.00
	$ 26,750.00

TOTAL BUDGET

$296,700.00

23 CLARA'S CLASSY COOKIES

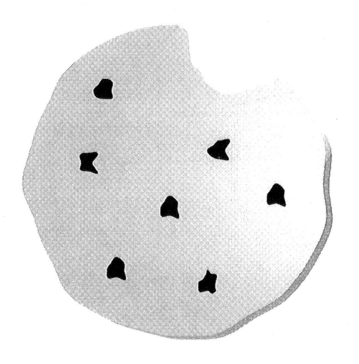

OVERVIEW: How to Expand a Fledgling Business

Clara Cooke had a great idea. Every holiday she baked an old family recipe for cookies—Chocolate Razzmatazz. (Her grandmother was a flapper and once danced the blackbottom with Al Capone. She had inherited the Chocolate Razzmatazz recipe from **her** grandmother.) Clara's personal contact and warm, friendly, magnetic personality enhanced the taste of these tasties. She sold them at bake sales, at cake sales, at Founder's Day, Guy Fawkes Day, Bastille Day, Arbor Day, any day, etc. Success, time after time! Clara's great idea was to market her cookies. Simple? Not at all! Clara initially made an arrangement with a local boutique to supply cookies and before you knew it, her cookies were all over the region. She called them **Clara's Classy Cookies**: Chocolate Razzmatazz, Strawberry Yummies, Snakerino Almond and Vanilla Wholly Molie cookies. People were falling all over themselves to buy **Clara's Classy Cookies** "in the plain brown wrapper." What to do next? How to expand this idea? So she decided to capitalize on this great idea.

Clara went to a nearby business-to-business advertising agency. Their resulting plan was brief and basic–perhaps too basic:

1. Advertise with full pages in the local *PennyPusher* publication, distributed free of charge to mailboxes in 17 different segments across the state.

2. Advertise in *News & times*, the dominant newspaper of the region on Wednesdays, (Wednesdays are "food" days here in Imaginaryland).

3. Use *Que-Pons Today*, the local direct mail coupon service with a coupon ad featuring a baker's dozen for each dozen cookies purchased. *Que-Pons Today* is distributed free to all on the 17 segment list.

4. Use the *Welcome New Homeowner* direct list for the entire state and mail to it.

5. Back it all up with a drive time-based 30 sec. spot on radio station WWII urging listeners to "call this number for a free sample of **Clara's Classy Cookies.**"

6. Dump the plain brown wrapper.

Well, Clara was no dumb cluck and hadn't built this profitable, albeit small business by accident. She wiped away the crumbs of a Snackerino Almond. *"I'm going to get a few optional plans,"* she told the president of the ad agency *"because I need to be right the first time and I want to work smarter, not harder."* She spouted several other clichés and was on her way

So she called a brand new firm, "XYZ Marketing Corp. Ltd." Their plan was quite similar to the advertising agency's:

1. Instead of *PennyPusher* full page print ads, XYZ recommended the use of their #1 competitor, *DollarDaze* with full-page print ads. They're cheaper per insertion so "you can get 35% more frequency."

2. Use the newspaper *Daily Dailies*, which has a food section on Thursdays, and a wider geography than *News & Times.* The cost is just about the same.

3. Use *Que-Pons today* direct mail service, just as the ad agency directed, but use twice as often.

4. Use *Ship Shape Shopper* vs. *Welcome New Homeowner.* It's half the price, with two-thirds the circulation.

5. Buy the billboard on the hill as you enter town off Route 5 and paste up a "**Clara's Classy Cookies,** 15 miles ahead" to cinch up the local business.

6. Don't use radio station WWII since cookies are a visual temptation. Use TV station XXX with flash blurb 15-second spots showing kids, teens, adults, and grandparents biting into over-

sized cookies, turning to the cameras and shouting: *"Yummmmmm classy taste. This must be a Vanilla Wholly Molie from **Clara's Classy Cookies**, 101 Main Street in downtown Bugaboo...made with the finest ingredients...what else would you expect from a classy cookie? Get a free sample at **Clara's** now. 101 Main Street, Bugaboo."*

7. Open a second location that distributes, but does not bake cookies on the premises.

8. Open one new location in year one, a second in year two, five more in year three and franchise each operation.

9. Dump the plain brown wrapper.

Clara was stunned as she wiped away the remnants of a few Pineapple Princesses with Acadamia Nuts cookies (they appealed to the local college crowd from Bugaboo U.). *"One source tells me how to advertise my business,"* she reasoned *"and the other tells me how to advertise it, plus how to be a franchise manager. And still others tell me to sit back and enjoy the fruits of my labor, and they said that with a relatively straight face. Hmmm. These all contain parts of what I want to do...but not anywhere near all of what I want to do...or how to set up to do it."* She smiled as an idea flipped off her spatula like a giant Space Spice 'n' Raisin, her newest creation. *"Maybe I'll call those guys that keep calling me...those schmoes or smees, or smoos or whatever they call themselves.* (She meant SMOs!) *I have their latest letter somewhere...."*

And the rest, though not history, is certainly historical.

Enter the Jones Boys

When the telephone rang at Jones, Jones & Jones Strategic Marketers, they were excited to receive Clara's call. After all, they were cookie lovers (who isn't? And they had pursued her for some six months already). But Clara was a tougher cookie than they anticipated. Even though she had the dough, she wanted to mix together all the right ingredients, add a little spice, and get her full measure's worth, develop the best recipe for success without wilting in the heat or sacrificing the icing on the...er...cake. So she asked the toughest question first. The conversation went a lot like this:

Clara: *"I'm Clara from **Clara's Classy Cookies** and I'm looking for some advice."*

Jones #1: *"We're big fans of your cookies, Clara. What advice are you looking for?"*

Clara: *"How to market my business."*

Jones #1: *"Well, you've come to the right place."*

Clara: *"Well, actually I've come to four or five places."*

Jones #1: *"I see. Why include us?"*

Clara: *"Well, I'm not completely satisfied with the recommendations I've received from the others...and I have to ask you one very important question."*

Jones #1: *"What's that?"*

Clara: *"What in the world is a schmoe?"*

Jones #1: *"That's SMO...Strategic Marketing Organization."*

Clara: *"Sounds great but what makes it so special?"*

Jones #1: *"It's different from traditional marketing and ad agencies."*

Clara: *"How so? I mean I don't need a cookie cutter company, no pun intended."*

Jones #1: *"The SMO is like an ad agency in that it **MIGHT** include* *advertising in its program...but might not. The ad agency invariably will, making it less objective and less concerned with your business."*

Clara: *"What about a marketing firm?"*

Jones #1: *"SMOs do incorporate many, if not all, of the functions of a marketing firm...but our recommendations are not necessarily limited to these. Also SMOs do not want to rep your product or develop a plan and then bow out."*

Clara: *"What about strategic marketing consultants vs. the SMO? What's the difference?"*

Jones #1: *"The strategic marketing consultancy does precisely that...develop strategic long-term plans for your products and/or business...and so does the SMO. The strategic marketing consultancy also will include a tactical or short-range plan. So does the SMO. And the strategic marketing consultancy may also provide some degree of tactical, hands-on business advice...whereas the SMO **always** provides some degree of tactical, hands-on business advice."*

Clara: *"That's it? That's the difference?"*

Jones #1: *"No. There's a much bigger difference. The SMO is staffed with professionals who are business people...who can fully coordinate all efforts...and **implement** the custom-designed plan...regardless of what it takes."*

Clara: *"I see."*

Jones #1: *"In other words, the business marketing plan is **never** second to anything else...not an advertising plan, a P.R. plan, or a direct mail campaign. Business is always primary with an SMO...and you have a single, focused point of contact for all efforts."*

Clara: *"Now that makes sense!"*

And so a lovely marriage was consummated. Here's how the plan was devised.

THE 15-POINT CHECKLIST

1. Who will service the account?

2. How do I know they'll work hard for me?

3. Experience?

4. Can they understand?

5. Can they learn?

6. Will they be there?

7. Can they handle all aspects of my account effectively?

8. Stability?

9. Controlling costs and charges.

10. Competition?

11. Aren't these steps a lot of trouble?

12. How do I measure their effectiveness?

13. What if they can't do it all?

14. What other factors should I consider?

15. A contract?

Only 15 Points?

Even Woodrow Wilson had 14 points. Clara went through the 15 points with the SMO firm of Jones, Jones & Jones. She asked, they answered.

1. Who will actually service the account?
Jones #1.

2. How do I know they'll work hard for me?
Time will tell, but the degree of their preliminary research and general recommendation helped convince her.

3. Experience?
Some retail, some baking industry. Much experience in distribution, which was where Clara knew she had to head.

4. Can they understand?
Clara pulled no punches, asked tough questions. Jones, Jones & Jones didn't avoid the answers. Gave opinions even when they seemed negative. Then came back and assaulted Clara with questions about her own business...then more questions, then still more. Whew!

5. Can they learn?
Clara checked out their client references including "E. P. Bushmaster & Co.," "Sky Country Health Center," and *"Frimmels Are Us."* Jones, Jones & Jones checked out very positively.

6. Will they be there?
Again the client's recommendation was very positive.

7. Can they handle all aspects of my account effectively?
Clara listened to their presentation, sifted out the obligatory superlatives, awards, etc., and felt comfortable with what she saw and heard.

8. *Stability?*
Banks, D&B all checked. Clara was doing thorough homework.

9. *Controlling costs and charges.*
Every item they showed was questioned for costs, including cost of production, creative, film, printing, dissemination, etc. Clara anticipated having no surprises and found out about media, fulfillment, and in general how they worked and handled accounts. A comfy zone was emerging.

10. *Competition?*
No, they had never worked for Clara's competitors. But then again, no one was quite a competitor, not the average bakery or Nabisco. Uniqueness was something Clara counted on.

11. *Aren't these steps a lot of trouble?*
Hardly. Clara's fortune was intertwined with this company or another like it. Why rush?

12. *How do I measure their effectiveness?*
A huge question. Clara and Jones #2 worked out the answer quite simply...via a full-scale strategic marketing plan with tactical probes. This meant that just selling more cookies wasn't enough...and the SMO had an entirely different venue to pursue...but we're getting ahead of ourselves.

13. *What if they can't do it all?*
At some point, Clara realized, she might outgrow the firm! But she bet dollars to donuts that it wouldn't happen for a number of years, and the SMO responded with a contingency precisely for that.

14. *What other factors should I consider?*
Like it says in the book,"anything and everything." And Clara did. From their location to their business philosophy to plans for their own future. She liked what she heard. And so she made her decision.

15. *A contract?*
Contract done, drawn, signed, sealed, delivered.

CHARTERING
CLARA'S CLASSY COOKIES

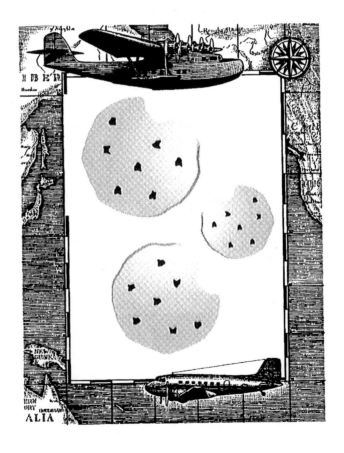

First You Start With...

Jones, Jones & Jones did their homework well. It was their nature. In addition to intensive strategic research into company, service, and product (which accounted for weight gains averaging 4.5 lbs. per Jones), the SMO developed a scenario that was at once comfortably predictable and strangely different. The first recommendation would warm the cockles of any SMO's heart. *"Keep the plain brown wrappers."* But the SMO presented the plan in a strategic form.

Jones Jones & Jones
strategic marketers

IDENTIFYING OUR TARGET AUDIENCES

The overall target audience for our cookies and related products is broad and highly diverse. Though it is well-suited for the "price is no object" consumer of premium cookies, reasonable pricing opens the product to the true mass market. Additional markets will be screened, evaluated, and opened as time goes on, particularly in the health area. We recommend two new markets to be targeted for immediate penetration: fat-free cookies and dietetic, no-sugar cookies. These food areas are booming. Examination of new products provides conclusive proof that these are currently active and expanding markets. Forecasts defining the health-conscious and the "over 40" market indicate that both segments will grow, stimulating demand, into the twenty-first century. We need to take advantage of these factors. The timing is right.

Jones Jones & Jones
strategic marketers

IDENTIFYING OUR GEOGRAPHIES

Our promotional efforts for year one will be confined to the United States, Canada, and Puerto Rico. Our focus will be national in the sense that we will seek profitable sales in all areas. Depending on which strategic avenues we elect to pursue in year one, we may or may not also promote product on a regional basis. Explanations follow.

Test marketing will take place in four recommended site areas: Austin, Texas; Tampa, Florida; San Diego, California; and Northern New Jersey.

IDENTIFYING OUR PRODUCTS AND SERVICES

Our product lines consist of the following:
Regular Cookies
Academia Nut
Chocolate Razzmatazz
Snackerino Almond
Strawberry Yummies

Oversized Cookies
Gigando Hodgepodge

Fat-Free Cookies
Berry Goods
Chocolate Razzmatazz

Dietetic Cookies (proposed)
Orange Essences
Vanilla Wholly Molie

HiCal SuperCookie Snax (proposed)
Mighty Mites
Turbo Nut Fudgies

Jones Jones & Jones
strategic marketers

IDENTIFYING THE COMPETITION

On the local level our research has located 16 competitors, including the well-established "Hernando's Bakery." On the regional level, supplying delis, food shops, diners, and other bakeries for resale, there are 36 companies, only one of which specializes in cookies (Big Mike's Mighty Moose Delicacies). Supermarkets are another type of competitor. Regional chains have recently penetrated the market locally. Product is made on premises 38% of the time, at another supermarket branch location, 26.5% of the time, and supplied outright 35.5%. At this juncture, there are no other visible competitors re: gourmet products.

LOCAL COMPETITION
ARMANDO'S
AU CHOCOLATE
DELICIOUS DELICACIES
GEHRINGER'S
HERNANDO'S BAKERY
HOT SPOT
HUNGARIAN PASTRY SHOP
JOHN'S BAKED GOODS
LE PATISSERIE
LE PETITE
OVEN FRESH
RUBENSTEIN'S BAKE SHOP
THE CONFECTIONERY
THE RAILWAY BAKERY
TREATS 'N' TRUFFLES
YE OLDE BAKERY SHOPPE

SUPERMARKETS
ABC MARKETS
METROGOTHAM FOODS
APEX MARKETS
VEGGIELAND
XYZ MARKETS

REGIONAL LEVEL COMPETITION
ALPHA ORDER CONFECTIONS
BIG MIKE'S MIGHTY MOOSE DELICACIES
BUGABOO BAKERY CORP.
HEAVENLY HOUR BAKERY SUPPLY
LARRY'S COOKIE WORLD
MARGIE'S CREATIONS

However, a close up look at the SMO's actual recommendations provided a surprise...a recommendation **not** to compete with these players...but to go...national? Clara was stunned. She read on and the plan began to click.

Why not compete? "**Clara's** has better products," she thought. "They have a more pleasing aroma. They look better, taste better. They **ARE** better. Better ingredients by far. Why not compete? But national? Why? How can that work?" "*How can that work?*" she asked.

"*Read on,*" Jones #1 said confidently.

Jones Jones & Jones
strategic marketers

MARKET GOALS: CLARA'S CLASSY COOKIES

We cannot sugarcoat our recommendations. We do not envision a sweet future for **Clara's Classy Cookies** at the local retail level. Costs will rise too high for any real returns. The horizontal expansion of the company to open new branches thwarts the entrepreneurial spirit in the sense that an entire hierarchy will need to be created, not merely to produce, but to market. Further, the market is limited in scope and the competition is firmly entrenched. The same is true (even truer!) on the regional level where business-to-business supply is dominated by two highly successful companies (Big Mike's and Bugaboo Bakery Corp.) who enjoy great reputations, have quality products, respectable pricing, popular promotional campaigns, established names, and solid, time-honored lines of distribution.

To engage these established businesses for market share with a head-on frontal assault would require an inordinate amount of time, energy, and capital, not to mention more luck than anyone is entitled to. Creating a groundswell demand at consumer level would also require considerable outright dollar expenditures plus personnel that **Clara's** currently does not have, and this still provides no guarantees of success. We have recommended a change in "menu and venue" for **Clara's Classy Cookies** in the following ways:

(1)   Product Line Expansion
By reviewing our product identification, you will see that we have recommended line extension to enter other markets that will bear fruit. Essentially these are personal health-related:

(a) Fat-Free Cookies.
(b) Dietetic Cookies.
(c) Hi-Calorie Cookie Snax.

These market niches need little explanation. The concern about heart and circulatory health, and high cholesterol levels have led to the fat-free market which is booming across the USA and Canada. Some 106 new fat-free food products of all types have been introduced in the last 60 days alone.

As the baby boomer generation ages, fat-free will become a way of life. Dietetic cookies (those with no sugar) have been a mainstay for years. The sales records of both Big Mike's Mighty Moose Delicacies and Bugaboo Bakery Corp. include substantive proof of success in these areas: 18% of total sales and 11% of total sales respectively. There is a large niche market here.

Jones Jones & Jones
strategic marketers

The Hi-Calorie Cookie Snax are directed to athletes and persons serious about their daily workout regimens. This is a burgeoning, growing marketplace entered recently by some very large international corporations. Our entry will have to be extremely well targeted and timed, and the caloric content and amount in Hi-Calorie Cookie Snax must be superior to the competition.

Regarding product line expansion and diversification, if the quality of **Clara's Classy Cookies** can be maintained, if all FDA and state guidelines can be met, if all distribution channels can be opened and used, **Clara's Classy Cookies** can become a large financial and artistic success.

26 IT'S OK TO BE SKEPTICAL

Skeptics of the World Unite—Now!

Clara was skeptical. Sure, she could create the correct recipes, and certainly she knew the cookies would have the right tastes, textures, etc. In fact she already had the final recipes for two of the three new offerings. But what was the SMO recommending if not local or regional sales? How was she to market nationally? And Jones #1 had a one-word answer that she had never expected.

"Catalogs," he said matter-of-factly.

Clara winced. "Catalogs? I'm going to put my cookies in catalogs?"

"Yes," he said. "In other people's catalogs as *Clara's Classy Cookies*, also as a private label, and most important, through your own speciality and master catalogs."

Clara grinned. "But what about financing?"

"We know you have backers...but here are the banks that are interested, with the appropriate names and phone numbers."

"But what about licensing and regulations?"

"We can recommend a legal firm that specializes in such matters. They are Smith, Smith & Smith. Here's their address and phone number."

"Lay the rest out for me."

"First we approach the established catalog marketers. 'The Sharper Vision,' 'Brands End,' 'Humma Schlumma,' 'Sillman Stonoma,' etc. Here are a list of names, positions, phone numbers, etc."

Clara nodded. "What about private labeling?"

"Again, that's a service we will offer to the catalog houses... putting their own brand names on our Gigando Hodgepodges or Strawberry Yummies. It makes sense."

"And, we could create new cookies for them and special packages...tins," Clara muttered, lost in thought.

Jones #1 smiled. "right. But the biggest market remains direct mail from **Clara's Classy Cookies** direct to the consumer."

Clara frowned. "Don't people get sick and tired of catalog after catalog piling up in their mailboxes?"

"Yes," Jones #1 answered. "That's why we're not going to do a direct mail catalog."

Clara frowned. "I'm just a small town baker. But I hear double-talk."

"No double-talk. We're going to do a direct mail **newsletter**...and here's the rationale."

Clara's Classy Cookies Newsletter: Strategic Marketing

The first step in crating a truly effective two-way communications newsletter is to ask a few questions.

1. Do I really need a newsletter?
2. Why not hit my audience with direct mail?
3. What should I expect from such a vehicle?
4. Will I control my newsletter or will my newsletter control me?
5. How do I know it's worth the time, effort, and money?

The manner in which we develop and handle newsletters makes answers become self-evident:

1. The need?

The need for a **Clara's Classy Cookies** newsletter clearly exists. Why? It demonstrates concern...adds continuity...offers a vehicle for on-going, two-way communication...establishes a position of stability...and it offers an ideal selling forum. We believe that this newsletter must be a prestigious, first-class effort, one carefully designed, written, and crafted to excellence, as befits an organization of **Clara's Classy Cookies'** stature...and the stature of its representatives.

2. Why not direct mail?

Newsletters in the true sense, **are** direct mail of a sort...but good, targeted newsletters are far superior to mundane, sales-oriented products all too often deemed "junk mail." Our newsletter will be a **highly personalized**, select vehicle which welcomes readers...and will be welcomed by them in turn. Our **Clara's Classy Cookies'** newsletter will say to the recipient in words, in graphics, and in concept, *"I contain information that you'll find useful or informative or* *thought-provoking. I'm from **Clara's** with love and I'm part of our personalization and commitment to you. And by the way, here is our wonderful product offering."*

Direct mail, since it is usually solely of a highly solicitative nature, does not have the interest nor the public relations value of a newsletter. It will not create the rapport and respect with **Clara's** audience that is crucial to long-term success. Our newsletter will.

3. What SHOULD someone expect from a newsletter?

Recipients expect items of interest...benefits...news. They hope for details, style, answers, data, solutions, incisive thoughts, "inside" information, "what's going on at **Clara's**," etc. They enjoy **PERSONALITY**, something **Clara's** has in abundance. They also expect an incisive offering of choice products. They **do not** expect or welcome corporate dogma, or *War and Peace*, or ultra-hip, trendy, but useless "inspirational" messages. **Clara's** newsletter will supply the message to answer real needs on the part of real recipients.

What should **Clara's** expect from a newsletter like this? RESPONSE! READERSHIP! APPRECIATION OF COMMITMENT! And most of all, favorable recognition and retention of **Clara's**...**Clara's** the company, **Clara's** the product, **Clara's** the service. Plus a fuller understanding of what makes the company clock tick...in other words, "a more perfect" environment. And that translates to superior communication, willfully "captive" repeat business and more — and easier — sales.

4. Control!

Control is what a newsletter offers most strongly. Apply strategic marketing and we leave nothing to chance. The SMO will control all timing, frequency, content, and style plus approaches, database, telemarketing, recipients, etc. This elevates the prospect of more timely production, immediate acceptance, quicker recognition, and faster reliance. As the regularity of publishing is established, our recipients will become Pavlovian and will look forward to receiving each newsletter...and each new offering of our delicacies.

5.*Bottom-lining: How do I know it's worth the time, effort, and money?*

Is it worth the time? Always, so long as it is done efficiently and professionally. **Is it worth the effort?** Handled professionally, yes. Handled arbitrarily, haphazardly, or treated as a secondary or tertiary consideration, no. Professionalism is the only way. This is the way to greater business. **Is it worth the money?** The proof's in the ...er...pudding. This is a sales vehicle. Whether it's from direct phone orders, catalog coupon returns, associated telemarketing sales, MasterCard or Visa orders, etc., **Clara's** will become known and established. The first time someone says *"I was reading in your newsletter and I want to order..."* then you'll have the answer and never question it again.

6.*Mind-share. Is no news good news?*

In marketing, particularly in tough economies, that adage is the first deadly sin. Anytime one communicates, it can result in new or better business, new or better commitment, new or better recognition. Waiting around for business to happen doesn't pay the bills, but communication will help earn mind-share...keep purpose in the thoughts of recipients...without being obnoxious. Regular communication keeps you into the race...and keeps you winning.

7.*The mosquitoes of marketing: An invasion of privacy?*

It is vital to keep in mind that even a great newsletter, like all direct mail, is an invasion of privacy. If you do not agree, you must be the sender. Once a newsletter is established, readers do welcome them as they no longer view them as annoying, invasive, and akin to mosquitoes. Strategic analyses makes the answer simple: make the transition gap as short as possible. How? By establishing the newsletter's beneficial position from the beginning...by making a commitment to greater frequency...as well as by better "quality" of content.

8.*Frequency or how much can I take?*

Frequency of issue is a very serious concern. Assuming that all input is informationally and categorically sound, it is natural to suppose that the greater the frequency the better. Unfortunately experience shows that's not always the case. No audience, no matter how interested, wants to receive a newsletter every day...or even every week...or in many cases every month. It's too much of a good thing at best...and nuclear devastation at worst. On the production end, it could be a nightmare for **Clara's**, and Jones, Jones & Jones, the implementor. We recommend a monthly frequency...with a provision for a "special issue" designated around a holiday or event, which would likely be of a lesser number of pages.

9. The best size! A most personal question.

We could debate the value of different sizes: "Typical" sizes range from 7" x 10" to 8 1/2" x 11" to 6" x 9" to 3 1/2" x 5" to supertab 12" x 16". However, considering our potential volume of information, the potential means of distribution, etc., we would recommend keeping **Clara's** newsletter in relatively standard sizes. After all, it's the message not the medium that we are relying on. We will distribute this in "coordinated" envelopes bearing the appropriate logos and messages. The SMO recommended a 16-page book-type newsletter for sales maximization.

10. Color! Color! Color! And taste!

Temptation...sweet temptation is involved in our offering and color images make the difference between a chocolate chip cookie...and a chocolate chip delicacy bursting with luscious morsels that melt in your mouth, are frèsh and crisp, etc. Colors should virtually explode off the page in support of each article's direction and purpose and each cookie's taste and look and texture. This doesn't mean we're choosing to create a chaotic color cornucopia or any such alliteration...but it does mean we will place a premium on the strategic use of color to help promote our overall intention and position. Four color is the way to go.

And then there are the other senses. One of the most attractive aspects of buying a premium cookie delicacy is the aroma. With impregnated strips, potential patrons can "sample" Orange Essences and "taste" the light, citrus snack by scratching an area in the newsletter. An aromatic appetizer can go a long way toward creating a customer...and the impregnation will be within our budgets.

11. True sampling.

Is there any more certain way to have someone buy the product than to have someone taste it? There is no better way! Test marketing by sample needs to be done. A business reply card via our newsletter can make it happen.

12. Writing, editing, and wordsmithing.

The SMO is, of course, fully capable of writing and editing all parts of the newsletter. It has been our experience that clients who insist that they will **PROVIDE** "original final" copy (how's that for an oxymoron?) are either stargazers or running for office...it never happens that way. Moreover, editing, whether it means knitting a list of disjointed thoughts into a cohesive, purposeful **INTELLIGIBLE** structure...or anglicizing someone's allegedly pristine allegory to render the other 99% of the universe capable of following it...is vital. Moreover, we know that **Clara's** can generate some articles of interest particularly technical ones, on a regular basis. However, Jones, Jones & Jones, with professional copywriters and editors, needs to be the major source of all items.

13. Creative control: Who's the boss?

The end defines (not justifies) the means. A strategic marketing organization, while not **Clara's** employees per se, are part of what Konosuke Matsushita termed "the extended business family." The SMO will value being valued and will not accept being "another vendor." Creative control, i.e., the final say so...will always rest in the hands of **Clara's** editor. However, the SMO's direction in terms of art, style, scheduling, etc., should be given all due consideration...and then some.

14. A single point of contact.

When the inmates run the asylum, it's time to close the facility. Having too many people with final say dealing with the production staff is about as safe as Hurricane Andrew or the San Francisco earthquake. A single point of contact on the client side...or final authority vested in his/her representative...is utterly necessary to ensure a successful newsletter program. As of now, it must be Clara.

15. *Production: Getting the job done.*

Once a single point of contact is established on the client side, it's vital to establish regular pre- and post-production meetings. Since Jones, Jones & Jones produces a good number of very complex newsletters, we are extremely proficient at scheduling. We will meet with **Clara's** selected editor immediately upon notification and begin scheduling for the first two issues.

CLARA'S CLASSY COOKIES NEWSLETTER:
A LOOK INSIDE

News! News! News!

Jones, Jones & Jones provided an overall scenario for the recommended newsletter/sales piece, including a computer-generated four color layout designed to knock socks off the proverbial ankles. It did. However, never put the tactic ahead of the strategy. It makes words like "justification," "rationalization," and "defensive" come out quite often in mixed conversation. The Jones Boys did what a good SMO would do...presented wonderful, beautiful, exciting, sizzling graphics...step four...preceded by strategic marketing...step two.

Jones Jones & Jones
strategic marketers

The Clara's Classy Cookies Newsletter: A Look Inside

Style and Design

We will create a clean, friendly, distinctive graphic look, one that immediately establishes purpose, objectives, and feel. The need is vital. **Clara's** newsletter will come across as super-professional, not spur-of-the-moment, not frivolous, never haphazard, or anything less than cutting edge. Our look will be fetching, attractive, even mouth-watering. It will make the recipient pick up the telephone and order...or return the order form...or be receptive to the telemarketer when he/she calls. We will come across as an ultra-professional, helpful newsletter, not merely as the sales vehicle we really are. Is this misleading? Not at all. We are providing a straightforward product offering to the public...plus helpful information and interesting bits and pieces.

We will translate all **Clara's Classy Cookies'** superior qualities. Graphics are ultra-modern. Page layout and columnation are crisp, clean, and copy-responsive, not copy-intensive. We are not limited by the use of a single typeface. Photos, art, icons, etc., are used as feasible to convey the message of each article column...as well as to image-enhance at every turn. We want superior readership and retention...and have designed everything to accomplish this.

Two Years Before the Masthead: *"Sweet Tidings"*

We see *"Sweet Tidings,"* our newsletter, as **A TRUE PUBLICATION**, deserving of a reader's time, effort, and appreciation. Anything less minimizes potential results. Our masthead professionalizes this newsletter and indicates our intent and commitment. It demonstrates from the very first instant that this is a publication worthy of being received...not yet another piece of junk mail. The *"Sweet Tidings"* masthead designates volume and issue, issue dates, issue frequency, etc. It is promissory in nature. It establishes the name of the periodical, a central theme to follow, and produces a feel of importance. We need this type of direction from the outset to be considered a serious contender. Our legend also reflects this.

$\mathcal{J}ones\mathcal{J}ones\&\mathcal{J}ones$
strategic marketers

Content and Personality

We recommend columnation to be employed wherever possible. By this we mean the organization of thoughts rather than the physical property. Columns **DO NOT** have to appear in every issue...but continuity is a positive thing. We have suggested several columns and will work directly with the **Clara's** editor to establish primary and secondary columns, as well as contingency sections and sidebars.

Copy, of course, has been created and edited. Copy will be informative and appropriately conversational. Newsletters should be **LOOSE!** They're friendly in nature as well as being helpful...copy should follow suit, but generally speaking, "the less, the better," so long as the proper points are made.

Personality is vital. We have replicated the nuances of personality that made **Clara's Classy Cookies** successful to begin with...honesty, forthrightness, a fanatical belief that using only the best, pure natural ingredients is the perfect match for the people who munch on **Clara's Classy Cookies**. And of course, a lot of love.

A Word About Fulfillment and Printing

Printing must be done on a modern four- or five-color press, by a first quality shop with all bindery options. Fulfillment, the actual handling, stuffing, labeling, mailing, lead processing, follow up, etc., should be performed by a leading fulfillment house. We have recommendations for both.

Establishment of Policy Guarantee

As *"Sweet Tidings"* will contain and offer product, it's vital to include a product guarantee. We strongly urge the institution of a "money back, no questions asked" guarantee. Given our quality from recipe through receipt, we do not anticipate many problems; and a customer who takes the time and effort (and expense) to send back partially eaten or damaged cookies, is certainly someone we will want to keep as a customer. So a "no questions asked" guarantee makes sense, and so does *"Sweet Tidings"* since it is a primary agent of policy. State it clearly, boldly, and often, and stand behind it...always.

Jones Jones & Jones
strategic marketers

BUDGETS AND SCHEDULES

ELEMENT I: 1995 NEWSLETTER PRODUCTION

Complete production of 24-page, five-color self-mailing
newsletter with business reply card, Volume 1, Number 1
including concept, layout, design, copy, typography, art,
photography, retouching, stats, computer mechanical (per
issue $32,500.00).

　　12 original issues 1995　　　　　　　　**$390,000.00**

ELEMENT II: 1995 NEWSLETTER PRINTING

24 pages, five-color, including stock, bindery, varnish, saddle
stitching, die-cutting, etc., 50,000-75,000 pcs.

　　12 issues @ $22,612.00　　　　　　　　**$271,344.00**

　　### Fulfillment
　　Addressing, labeling, mailing

　　12 issues @ $8,000.00　　　　　　　　**$ 96,000.00**

ELEMENT III: LIST ACQUISITION
50,000-75,000 fully culled names　　　　　　**$ 12,760.00**

ELEMENT IV: LIST MAINTENANCE
Average cost per month, 12 @ $1,000.00　　　　**$ 12,000.00**

The Necessity of Good List Management

Mailing a professional, sales-oriented newsletter such as the one proposed herein, is not without timing, deadlines, and costs. Therefore, each newsletter must be mailed to prospects highly likely to become customers. Culling and managing prospect lists are vital activities. Constant on-line review, not periodic review, is necessary. Evaluation of prospect status should be done on a monthly basis if not sooner.

28 THE STARTING POINT

Starting Point? Aren't we nearly finished?

No. Naturally recognition and acceptance were vital to Clara's success...and that meant recognition and retention and appreciation of **Clara's Classy Cookies** (the company) and **Clara's Classy Cookies** (the brand) in addition to the actual cookies themselves. The SMO started at the beginning: a logo treatment. Eight are presented. Which one do you think Clara and the Jones boys selected?

Since this was the basic springboard design, the logo needed to be eminently flexible and versatile, highly memorable, and of course, classy.

Jones Jones & Jones
strategic marketers

CLARA'S CLASSY COOKIES INC.

Clara's Classy Cookies

Classy Cookies

Cookies inc.

Clara's classy cookies

The next step involved isolating all the elements that were considered important and placing them within a hierarchy. The SMO narrowed a major list to five:

1. a circular motif reminiscent of the commonly held ideal type of cookie.
2. something to indicate good taste.
3. a stylish, smooth, non-dating typeface.
4. reproducibility in both one color or four-color process.
   - (a) on letterhead, stationery, business cards, forms, etc.
   - (b) on metal tins of various sizes containing from one dozen to four dozen cookies.
   - (c) package design (three cookies) in a vending machine.
   - (d) on a catalog cover.
   - (e) in any variation of the newsletter itself, e.g., disk, CD-ROM, etc.
5. multiple applications orientation.
   - (a) on signage.
   - (b) on vans and trucks.
   - (c) on P-O-P displays.
   - (d) in advertising.

The SMO's art department returned with countless variations, then narrowed the selection to about a dozen. Before presenting to the client, the five points were applied. Two logos were eliminated as too "designy." Another was eliminated because it was considered "too, too classy." Yet another was limiting in typeface and another was too plain. Too current was also a consideration; what about next year? Another had a nice idea but seemed to reflect graham crackers, not cookies. One close, but more limiting than its sister design. Finally, others were eliminated because they were simply not classy enough in type style. So what did that leave? The following master logo.

It had the circular motif reminiscent of one logo and a stylish, smooth, non-dating typeface...plus color reproducibility, balance, readability on any number of applications. No "bite" (as in some logos) was taken out of the cookie, as several major competitors had already used that. Clara applauded.

Clara had a multitude of other questions, just like a good client should. She challenged. Jones answered. And satisfactorily. They proceeded. And finally they got close to the end.

FINALIZING CLARA'S PLAN

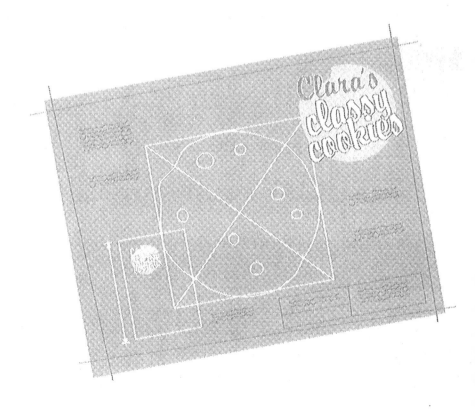

Getting There

In order to facilitate the acquisition of necessary investment dollars to provide proof positive and to minimize risks, Jones, Jones & Jones included measurement and evaluation devices in their proposal:

1. Strategic Taste Tests

Tastings would take place in selected, screened, qualified major buying ares that **Clara's** had never penetrated. These could be city segments, whole cities, urban and suburban areas, or regions across the board. They could be in-store, in-supermarket, kiosk-in-mall, in-mail, in-strip mall, etc. Key criteria required development but this was to be an on-going process for the product introduction. Audience identification and screening was essential. Catalog introduction by taste testers was also essential, requiring training.

2. Key Focus Group

In the true sense of a focus group, this measurement device would come into play some six to 12 months after product introduction. Certainly consumers cannot comment on cookie consumption until they've actually consumed **Clara's Classy Cookies**. this is more than an alliterative way of saying let's buy some time to get the product going. This really says we have to have the audience in place first...or else we're really just doing strategic taste testing all over again...at a great waste of dollars.

3. Trial Balloon Telemarketing

Telemarketing, being one of the most misunderstood marketing services available today, was typically misunderstood in its application to **Clara's Classy Cookies**. As Jones #3 explained to Clara, and later to Clara's bankers and backers, *"Telemarketing is not included in our definition of core business."* The bankers, ostensibly imbued with the spirits of reengineering, empowerment, and other snazzy au courant business terms, exclaimed in unison *"Then why are you recommending it? You are recommending it, are you not?"*

Jones #3 hesitated. Should he tell them the truth, tell them something they wanted to hear, or change the subject without them even realizing? He chose the second avenue.

"Telemarketing is not your core business. That seems simple enough. But like all forms of marketing, there is a natural attraction to doing it oneself."

"Yes. Then we **control** *it,"* a banker noted.

"Control your **core** *business, stay out of areas you don't know enough about to be an expert,"* Jones #3 retorted.

"Then what's the solution?" Clara interrupted.

"Hire a telemarketing service. Here's a non-exhaustible, rule-of-thumb list to consider."

A. **Field Survey:** Through or in conjunction with your SMO, learn what companies are active in the field. You can use the Yellow Pages, trade publications, or the advice of business acquaintances experienced with such services. But list and survey the potentials.

B. **Qualification:** Once a list of possible telemarketers is developed, it's time to qualify them. A complete set of guidelines and criteria should include the usual questions:

How long in the telemarketing business?
Company philosophy.
Who are your clients? Large ones, small ones?
Which clients have been with you the longest?
Number of employees?
Breakdown of employee duties.
Number of telemarketers?
Total volume?
Why are you different?
Special services.
Degree of computerization.
Typical fees.
Biggest success story. Why?
Biggest failure. Why?

C. **Basic Training:** No matter how much the companies interviewed waver, sidestep, apologize for, or gloss over, this is the single most vital factor in selecting a service. Training in all cases is continuous, or should be; it never stops. Do not settle for anything but crystal clear answers to the question *"How and how long do you train your people?"* Regardless of what they say, extract the truth. If they give you answers of arbitrary time, i.e., days, weeks, months, wave bye-bye. They're missing the point. There is no substitute for on-going, continuous training. Accept no less.

D. Performance Monitoring: How does the client learn how things are going along? What's the reporting structure? What type of reports? How is everyone monitored? How often?

E. Flexibility of Program: Assuming that training is continuous, what mechanisms exist to introduce new concepts or items or sales points? In other words, if a new sales point is uncovered or realized, how is it introduced to the telemarketing team? Why is this an effective way to go? How do you know the staff has gotten the point?

F. Results Reporting: How are results made available? In what time span? Hourly? Daily? Minute-by-minute?

G. Validation of the Plan: How long will it take to determine whether the plan itself is viable? How about the viability of the product? Make sure you receive clear, concise answers before venturing forth, not *"Well I guess we could,"* or *"This should be ..."* And get it in writing.

H. Don't do it yourself: Think professional. Think results. Think clear-cut answers. Don't muddy the waters by getting involved and trying to telemarket yourself. It's not your **core** business. Don't try to fix your toothache yourself. Let your SMO find the right professional telemarketing team for you. And then hire them. Fast! It is very tempting to try to telemarket internally. Ask your SMO first. They'll tell you the pros and cons of doing it yourself.

After Clara and the bankers had digested the SMO's recommendations and measurement devices, they appeared to be dubious. Jones #2 exhaled loudly. *"So you need more convincing? What's your* **core** *business? Why spend all your time doing this IF a service can do it to relatively the same success factor?"*

"But I control it," Clara volunteered.

"No," Jones said. *"Then it controls you. Don't build an empire, build your business."*

Jones, Jones & Jones' recommendation was to use a telemarketing service at least in the early stages. Why? Cost, professionalism, timing. Then Clara and the bankers would see how well they do it...and not try to butt in and do it themselves. Don't ask a cat to bark, or a dog to purr.

In the specific case of **Clara's Classy Cookies**, telemarketing was considered as a trial balloon. The concept was to test a three product line spread (existing best seller, new fat-free, and new sugarless dietetic cookies) as well as the program of small catalog, merchandising sales. The SMO developed and formulated the necessary criteria, putting it in place so that it was ready to go.

30 TRADE SHOWS

To Trade Show or Not to Trade Show

The central focus in the issue of trade shows is always whether to just attend, or to attend and display? The SMO recommended to display, in an effort to notify and promote the sale of goods. So what next? Which shows? Locals? Regionals? Nationals? It all comes back to basic strategic marketing, the SMO insisted. Who are we trying to reach and influence and why?

Marketing through trade shows would work well for the private label segment of **Clara's Classy Cookies'** marketing plan. Trade shows bring the buying audiences together in close proximity with **Clara's** to:

1. give a visual impression of **Clara's** as a potential private label provider.
2. provide a sensual experience via product sampling.
3. offer a "best foot forward" first impression, as potential distributors and customers are visiting **Clara's** rather than vice versa.
4. offer an opportunity to showcase the company, and its creative and manufacturing qualifications, re: capabilities, facilities, commitment to quality, etc.
5. create a business environment, where business is expected.
6. enable **Clara's** to gauge market demand for its products as private labels, gauge potential market size and volume, etc.
7. see what key reps and distributors think of the product(s) and potentialities.
8. introduce new logos, art, package design, etc.
9. introduce new programs, spiffs, proposals, etc.
10. survey the competition.

So trade shows can be vital to the private label segment of **Clara's** business. However, they're a huge commitment, require much preparation, and key strategic and tactical marketing. The SMO suggested the following as a primer.

Jones Jones & Jones
strategic marketers

A trade show primer. Or, what do we want to achieve by trade show participation?

To be seen, of course! And noticed. And understood. And appreciated. And retained. No one goes to a trade show to hide...though all too often poor planning, poor design, poor position, and poor execution guarantee that this will happen. Jones, Jones & Jones treats shows as ultimately manageable and profitable entities that require careful planning, handling, and feeding to be productive. In order to determine the real needs of **Clara's Classy Cookies** and to make the design and utilization of a **Clara's Classy Cookies** trade show display both effective and cost-effective, we suggest the following categories of consideration, in a checklist for fast scanning:

1. Overall Intent and Purpose
2. Staffing
3. Physical
4. Product Considerations

Jones Jones & Jones
strategic marketers

1. Overall Intent and Purpose

- Do we want to encourage mass viewing or select viewing? Or both, depending on the specific show?

- Do we expect to walk away with business orders? With leads?

- Will each show lead subsequently be prequalified to separate real leads from literature gatherers, autograph seeking, or prize-seeking floor walkers? Will they be qualified by our salespeople or representatives?

- Will we have in-show promotions? Drawings? Prizes?

- Will we normally operate from a strategic position of strength in terms of our physical location?

- Is the nature of our organizational setup well known to attendees? To whom? Do we need to explain to any particular group?

- Is the interrelationship of our products known?

- Can we develop a hierarchy matrix matching show and attendees?

- Are all our products well known? Are any? Does the average attendee know our benefits?

- Is our corporate position well known? Do we need to tell the company story or re-enforce it?

- Are our product positions well known?

- Will we be appearing for the first time at any shows?

- Will all our products have "equal weight" at our top three shows?

- Will we have a regular hospitality suite?

- How will we differentiate between customers and "real" customers?

- Are we sponsoring any special seminars? Poster sessions? Meetings?

Jones Jones & Jones
strategic marketers

- Are we receiving any awards? Making any presentations?

- Should we survey the attendees at our booth?

- How will we effectively measure our show success for evaluation? By leads, by quality leads, by orders, by sales, by attendance, by surveys, etc.?

2. Staffing
- How many salespeople and/or representatives will we have at a given show? Will we need Clara there herself?

- What is the show hierarchy to be? How will we advise our people?

- What will the ratio of salespeople to attendees be?

- Will we use "models" or "greeters" to greet, welcome, fill out forms/entries, distribute literature? If not, who will handle such activities?

- Will our salespeople be proactive or reactive?

- Will our salespeople be show-trained?

- Will our entire staff require show sales training?

- In addition to capabilities and features, will our salespeople be free to talk pricing? Delivery? Availability?

- Will we have a designated show manager?

- Will the show manager be responsible for:

  a) staffing?
  b) time scheduling?
  c) outside functions?
  d) inside arrangements?
  e) communications?
  f) pre- and post-show evaluation meetings?
  g) union interaction?
  h) booth construction?
  i) other?

Jones Jones & Jones
strategic marketers

•Will the staff be fully advised of show regulations?
•Will we utilize pre-show mailers? Invitations?

3. Physical
   •Will we do our own move-in and setup/knock-down?
   •Do we need a dedicated conference area? Enclosed or open?
   •Do we require a tower of centralized focal area?
   •Do we require a theater? Remote video terminals? Interactive stations?
   Kinetic displays? Live stage? More than one tier?
   •How will we handle power, storage, seating, carpeting, lighting, plumbing,
   telephones, multiple levels?
   •Will we bake samples at the booth? What will we need to do this? Can we
   do this legally?
   •Will we require remote sampling stations?

4. Product Considerations
   •How well known are all our products?
   •Do all our products require in-booth sampling? How will we achieve this?
   •Are our products' markets well known to attendees?
   •How will we accommodate the sampling in terms of show traffic flow?
   •Do our product ingredients match up well with the competition?
   •How important is explaining our manufacturing process?
   •Which of our product lines require in-person explanation? Video
   explanation? Literature explanation?
   •Which products require table top areas for display? Backdrop displays?
   Display cases?
   •If we can bake in-show, which product(s) will we bake?
   •Will we have any technical demonstrations?
   •Which products will be active? In use as demos?
   •Will we have any technical explanations re: ingredients?
   •Will we require accessories for product demos, i.e., ovens, refrigerators,
   computers, microscopes, product enlargement models, etc.?
   •How often will we have new products? Major/minor?
   •Which lines are scheduled to have these new products? Short-term?
   Long-term?

Jones Jones & Jones
strategic marketers

- Will we introduce or preview new products at most shows? How will we handle this?
- Will we use shows as blind taste test areas for proposed new products?
- Will this be at the show, at the booth, at a hospitality suite, or done by "roamers"?
- Will shows form the launch foundation for our new products? What role will they play?
- Will we promote the in-show distribution of product literature?
- Will there be technical/abstract poster areas to be considered?
- Which products require specialized displaying areas?
- Do any of our products require stand-alone areas?
- Are any products extraordinarily oversized? Undersized?
- Will our competition be launching new products?
- How large a role will display modularity play in terms of space booked for various shows?
- What are the most common booth configurations we will require? What is the "worst case" or "weirdest" configuration?
- Are we aware of the normal life cycle of a display?
- How important will graphics be? Kinetics? Illumination?
- Which products will dominate which shows?
- Do we want free flow traffic? Directed (tour) or undirected traffic?
- Will we generally have separate hospitality areas at the show itself?
- Are any shows scheduled within two weeks of each other?

Jones Jones & Jones
strategic marketers

Strategic Recommendation

Attendance at Cookiefest North America and Patisserie Shop Expo are essential. Two other shows, Cookie Crumbles and American Fruit of the Oven Show, make sense. We will require a customized booth, no smaller than 10′ x 20′, likely to be 20′ x 20′. A tower is not recommended in these sizes. Cookiefest and American Fruit of the Oven permit in-show baking; the others prohibit it. Attendance is recommended at all four shows, though Patisserie Shop Expo does not currently merit a 20′ x 20′ size. A 10′ x 20′ will be sufficient. Through attendance, and display of products, services, and capabilities at these four key shows, **Clara's** will achieve excellent saturation for a first-time exhibitor.

 **ADVERTISING?**

TOM DUNNE

Advertising? Are you sure?

When the topic is advertising, suddenly everyone's an expert. Is it possible that there is one solitary individual living in the USA (or the world for that matter), who watches television, listens to radio, scans newspapers, studies magazines, reads books, or in any way is connected with mass media, **who is not an expert on the subject of advertising?** People who take subways to work and play are experts on the latest model cars. They can quote individual sales features, available financing, and prices at will, or tell you which has "rich Corinthian leather," the "Northstar System," or other exotic esoterica. Nursery school graduates can tell you everything you'd ever want to know about such adult subjects as hair restoral, PMS products, dating services, and land sales in areas they can't quite pronounce. People who haven't been to the movies in a generation or two can regale you with comments of leading critics for the latest and greatest in cinema. Those who dread shopping malls and supermarkets can tell you the best places to buy socks, shoes, and pants, who has the best buy on bananas this week, and what deli items cost the most per pound.

So what's the point? A simple one. We, as average individuals, receive thousands of advertising images and messages each day. Today, we as a people, are so over-inundated with ads, pitches, hype, special thises and thats, promotions, spots, advertorials, commercials, sales presentations, infomercials, etc., it's no wonder that most of us can hum McDonald's latest catchy ad campaign tune or the theme songs for our favorite major league teams...no wonder we can recite the current themes for virtually every mundane household cleaning product, or milk, or any of several cola drinks...but we cannot name more than three of the basic items in the Bill of Rights, can't recall even half the presidents of the USA, can't enumerate more than 35 states. It's no wonder we draw complete blanks at recalling the Declaration of Independence, the Gettysburg Address, or the beautiful, descriptive poetry on the Statue of Liberty...and it's no wonder we fumble, mumble, grumble through the "Star Spangled Banner" praying for brevity and wondering why our national anthem refers to a Georgia baseball team. Our brains are ad-ified!! Advertorialized! Commercially redundant! So to show the difference between the ad agency and the SMO, expect that the first questions the SMO will ask are different from that which the typical ad agency will ask.

AGENCY

(1) What advertising do I need to sell the product?

(2) How will my account react to my proposal?

(3) Will my account's advertising campaign stand out from the competition's?

(4) Do we need backup support literature?

(5) Have we missed anything?

SMO

(1) What are my client's end goals?

(2) What does my client require to do better business?

(3) Will our position be one that accurately reflects/supports my client's sales and marketing focus?

(4) Does my client need advertising or similar "reach vehicles" at all?

(5) Here's where the program begins and where it ends.

Then the smart SMOs begin by defining advertising and its very nature.

The Nature of Advertising

In today's business environment, there are few things as misunderstood as advertising. To some groups the term "advertising" evokes connotations of 60-second spots on National TV during the Super Bowl...to others, fractional page black and white print ads chockablock with type in local newspapers...to others humorous drivetime radio serial ads or six-page full-color inserts in business-to-business trade publications. Still others may see advertising as a 500,000 piece direct-to-end user direct mail campaign. One might ask, **"Who is correct?"** The answer? **"Everyone."**

Advertising, therefore, can assume many different forms. However, there is one thing that identifies and exemplifies all advertising — **it is an essential ingredient in the marketing mix!**

The SMO's Outlook

Advertising, to the SMO, is certainly not the whole enchilada...it might be the tortilla or the rice and beans...but it is only one promotional arm of marketing, albeit a powerful one...and it can create a great number of positive situations. But first, a potential advertiser must recognize what he or she **wants** to accomplish, and what he or she **realistically can** accomplish. Goals must be carefully determined and specified. Target audiences must be identified and placed in a "reach hierarchy." Strategies must be researched. Methodologies must be weighed, detailed, and evaluated. Then, and only then, **after a plan has been instituted**, should a company embark on an advertising venture...and then the company's public position has to be crafted, structured, created, instilled, and established.

Ask yourself: What do I want my advertising/promotional program to do?

Many executives, from CEOs to high, middle, and lower management, simply cannot decide on a workable answer to this question. Typically it requires an unbiased marketing professional, an SMO to wit, to effect an appropriate answer. Success must begin at this point, **by identifying what an advertising program is capable of doing for a company**...and proceeding from there.

The following points are tutorial in nature, and discuss six major attributes of advertising.

1. Mass Audience, Mass Message, Sales Booster

In a marketplace as vast as the USA, door-to-door selling of most products/services is virtually impossible and extravagantly expensive...especially in a business-to-business environment — unless sales are supported by an army of unpaid cookie-bearing young girls in cute green uniforms (with or without berets!). A strong, well-conceived advertising/promotional campaign will convey a company's distilled message to more people, more quickly, and more often...providing the product is available. How much advertising depends on the market dynamics and on how quickly a company wants to boost sales.

In many volatile markets, speed of sale is of the essence. Situations, like sovereign nations, rise and decline. Often the window of opportunity is open for only brief time spans. Simply having "good" products and "good" services doesn't guarantee that the market will be there when you want it to be, or that anyone will beat a path to your door.

Any salesperson worth his/her salt will tell you that being in the right place at the right time is the key to sales success. But how many accounts can one person visit in a single week? Advertising will never replace face-to-face selling...but it certainly supports and makes face-to-face selling easier and more effective.

The SMO observed that the marketplace for **Clara's Classy Cookies** had all the normal problems associated with any market — economies of scale, economies of demand, etc. There was also an unpredictable revolutionary trend — what was once the hottest product could be left high and dry and dusty — unsalable — on shelves six months later. And that could affect **Clara's** directly and direly. **Clara's** marketplace was also characterized by organizations extremely well entrenched...with company and product names the target audiences have grown to respect...rely on...and support. The SMO knew they would have to overcome these perceptions...and no vehicle informed mass audiences any better, any faster than well-targeted advertising.

2. The Friendly Persuader

One of the most difficult things to do in life is to change some-one's mind...and in business it's usually even tougher. For example, how do you influence a potential buyer's mind when he/she has pur-chased the same reliable equipment from the same reliable vendor for ten or 20 years? How do you change a potential end user's mind when he/she wants to buy one "tried, trusted and true" name brand vs. any other name brand? The answer can be advertising...a time-proven changer of buying habits.

Once upon a time in the USA, there was a familiar scenario called "Let's go siesta and let the competition steal our business out from under our sombreros." It usually happened in existing products, where one or two companies dominated. Virtual monopolies. When a new domestic or foreign competitor made inroads into this market dominance, the American manufacturers typically ignored the chal-lenge and went on with business as usual. The philosophy of "don't need the business," or its equivalent thrived. It happened in automo-biles, consumer electronics, steel, communications, even chocolate! The scenarios are remarkably consistent. The competition had equiv-alent or better products. They got the inside track by promoting an image of quality to a receptive new generation. They simply adver-tised it, promoted it...everywhere they could...at every opportunity. They didn't knock the established companies...didn't have to...just used "friendly persuasion." Once the foothold was significant, then they went for the jugular. The established companies reeled from the attack, lost substantial percentages of their marketshares before eventually getting smart and fighting back. What did they do? They advertised...heavily, with blitzes, both direct to consumer and direct to trade. Some regained much of their marketshares...and became more profitable than ever. Others...well they stayed afloat or went belly up; either way they never forgot their lessons. In this case, advertising spelled market interest and commitment to the audi-ences. It established quality positions. It established an attitude that each entire organization could rally around...and did...one that ever-changing consumers could recognize via a high visibility campaign.

3. Preselling vs. Impulse Selling

In conjunction with opinion alteration, a potential advertiser must always consider the question of **when** to advertise. Preselling means that when the potential purchaser is looking to buy he/she has already been exposed to the benefits of our products and services... and that **he/she already knows what he/she wants**

Assume this position: The potential purchasers are educated and advised of the salient points of a product or service. They know the benefits and advantages...and like as not, its disadvantages. When they receive budgets, they don't want soliloquies or novels...they want the product that best suits their needs...and they want it **NOW**. You might argue that this is a good case for impulse buying. It is. But a presold buyer is more likely to buy the product he/she was presold on...whether they buy it impulsively or not. Certainly there may be wining and dining involved, but if you're not already in the running, chances are you won't be considered. Since they are more apt to quickly purchase the intended product/service, they are, through line extension, far more likely to buy peripheral or related products/services in addition to their original purchase. With preselling, line extension can reap enormous sales rewards.

Impulse selling is designed to occur at the point of purchase "on the spur of the moment." It has major drawbacks, foremost being that the promoter has a tougher time selling the product/service because of a need to open, direct, and close **the entire sale right then and there**. The end user has been exposed only superficially. This puts unnecessary stress and weight on the seller, in particular the sales force, which has to hit a "homer"...do that in a huge ball-park...on the first pitch they see...from a pitcher they've never seen before...without much batting practice. Consumer ignorance and reluctance often spell **"NO SALE."** Also, impulse selling more often requires a hefty "boost"—point-of-purchase, on-site premiums/incentives/etc., which can erode profit margins.

Clearly, preselling is the superior way to go in terms of sales volume profitability; and **no vehicle is superior to establishing a preselling environment than advertising**. Advertising combines the mass audience/mass message tenet and the friendly persuader/preselling tenet to form one of, if not the most viable, sales avenues available in terms of the results-to-cost ratio. And this can make advertising a sales force's "best friend"...but that lead has to be established and followed.

4. Image Establishment and Reputation

Advertising creates image*...for products. for services, and for companies. Most school children realize this. Every ad, whether it is in a magazine, on TV, heard over the radio, or on a package, is a billboard...it says different things to different people...evokes different emotional responses...thoughts...ideas...actions; however, the key is to have that image be the most **positive one** possible, regardless of how it can be construed or misconstrued...and to reinforce the company's or product's position accurately. Regarding **Clara's** campaign, the SMO recommended product and service images to revolve around the advantages tied to the new products. They felt that it was vital to project the image of quality based upon **Clara's** taste, look, feel, capabilities, durability, etc.

The role of **Clara's** advertising was to enable the new organization to drive home cardinal tenets of its philosophy or position. Essentially, points like **reliability, dependability, honor, commitment,** and the most nebulous English word or all, **"QUALITY,"** can be treated so as to be readily associated with the name of the company and/or the product. This creates a real corporate "position" that once achieved, clarifies and improves all product sales...and makes new product introductions immediately more successful by "preselling" the product through the established integrity of the company.

This is an absolutely invaluable situation, a position of power and strength. No price tag can be put on establishing the value of the quality, the honor, the commitment of an organization such as **Clara's**; and advertising, because of its repetitive, reinforcing nature, was deemed by the SMO to be the vehicle best suited for establishing this in large, horizontal niches and vertical niche markets as well.

---

*The difference between "image" and "position" is substantial. Image is a feeling, a nuance, an inkling, an attraction, an instinctive association with, in this case, a company and product. Image is typically the external manifestation of a company's position, i.e., the facade exposed to the target audience. Positioning is a meticulously crafted, extremely detailed process which, among many other things, establishes image.

5. *You Can't Sell a Bad Product*

First of all, it's important to understand that a product can be "bad" for very good reasons: it can be ahead of its time...or behind its time. It can be mal-targeted, misunderstood, or obviously lacking in advantages. But no successful product or service is inherently "bad."

Everyone can think of a "bad" product that sold. Or can they? Pet rocks? No, this was not a bad product; it was a non-product. Moreover, it was promoted as such, given a light-hearted marketing slant, and it worked to great success. Then is success of a product the characteristic that keeps it from being bad? No.

In a marketplace like **Clara's**, "bad" and "good" products and services change through a product life cycle. What was once good can become less good. One aspect can alter others. Pistachio nuts were poor sellers until their white shells were dyed red. People loved them even if the dye came off on their fingers. Then as health concerns and the demand for "naturalism" arose, manufacturers eliminated the dye (despite the fickleness rampant in that the dye is never consumed). One batch of stale or malformed products can sink a brand, especially in "personal reward-oriented" products like cookies. The key is to establish the "goodness" quickly. Advertising does this on a mass basis by establishing the goodness, i.e., the end user advantages, right away, at first impact. No, you can't sell a "bad" product, but **Clara's** does not have "bad" products. **Clara's** standard products compare with anyone's and exceed every new one currently on the horizon...and the SMO's recommended advertising was designed to encompass that.

6. *We Don't Have to Advertise*

Advertising, as laboriously noted, is merely one form of promotion, one droplet in the sales flow and one chemical in the marketing mixture. More accurately it is a catalyst that makes a reaction occur. For **Clara's**, the SMO was seeking to make sales happen, not just for today but for as long as **Clara's** is in this business. The most serious reason to continually advertise is that every marketplace changes. How does one combat turnover? Can one effectively reach the 14% to 22% of the market that turns over every year by personal calls? Possibly...if one knows them...if one's sales force is large enough...dedicated enough...well-trained enough...if the market is small enough...if the new powers-that-be have recognized the need...if the new consumer is interested and open minded...etc. And there's still no guarantee of new or continued business.

Even if the turnover is only 12% per year, that's 13.4% turnover the second year, 15% the third year, 16.9% the fourth, and nearly 19% the fifth year. That's quite a bit to overcome. And who's to say that your sales force will remain the same...meaning new salespeople will have to establish new relationships anyway.

Then, by not advertising, is the 22% market share left victim to the competition's preselling efforts? **Of course!!!** So what image is now projected? To those who know the company, the products, etc., there is nothing necessarily new — we have not upgraded our image. If the target audience who knows us has perceived negatives previously, why would they assume that we have upgraded our products, service, support? Because the sales force is contacting them on a weekly basis? Monthly? Every six months? To those who don't know you, how will they ever get to know what you stand for? Every business is different, and the need for actual advertising varies. The SMO noted that in **Clara's** business, the competition advertised heavily. They recognized that media advertising provided many invaluable services...recognition, saturation, reach, targetability, comfort, etc...which is why Jones, Jones & Jones, strategic marketers, recommended a regular advertising program as a major thrust.

Jones Jones & Jones
strategic marketers

RECOMMENDED ADVERTISING

For all the preceding reasons, advertising as a vehicle doesn't make sense for **Clara's Classy Cookies**...and does.

POCKET ANALYSIS:
RECOMMENDED ADVERTISING

Jones #3 had a hard time defending this one to his audience (Clara, her newly hired internal marketing people, the bankers, and backers who put up the bucks, etc.). Finally, he gave up trying to give the full rationale and went to specifics. His card was as follows:

$\mathcal{J}ones\,\mathcal{J}ones\,\&\,\mathcal{J}ones$
strategic marketers

MARKET: Consumer

RECOMMENDED ADVERTISING TYPE: None

FREQUENCY: None

Pocket Analysis: This may seem oversimplified, but you can't get consumers to buy the product if the product isn't stocked and on the proverbial shelves. So no amount of advertising will work. It's premature at very best.

Jones Jones & Jones
strategic marketers

MARKET: Bakeries

RECOMMENDED ADVERTISING TYPE: Print Space

FREQUENCY: Monthly

Pocket Analysis: Advertise to other bakeries seeking a premier cookie line for resale. **Clara's** can offer quality plus competitive pricing and fast delivery. Future plans in this area would be to ship packaged frozen or refrigerated dough cut and formed for instant baking. Recommended print advertising, full pages, full color, 6X each in:

1.   Bake 'N' Shake World: monthly circ. 16,180.

2.   Cookie Crumbles Register: monthly circ. 22,455.

3.   Bake Shop Business: monthly circ. 20,007.

Theme: "No one knows your customers better."

Jones Jones & Jones
strategic marketers

MARKET: Hotels

RECOMMENDED ADVERTISING TYPE: Print Space/Direct Mail/ Telemarketing

FREQUENCY: Mixed

Pocket Analysis: As a branded product or as a private label, hotels need to supply quality products; and they have an audience that will spend premium dollars. Special sizing and portioning must accommodate the needs of the individual hotels. Direct mail must be used as teasers and door openers. Telemarketing should be used as the first and second follow-up. Print space advertising should be employed in the specific niche publications that reach the hotel buyers and food managers, themselves. Full page, full color is preferred.

1. Hotel Noshers Management: monthly circ. 37,500.

2. Reservations Please: weekly circ. 33,875.

3. Room Service Weekly: weekly circ. 34,415.

4. American Food & Beverage Honchos: weekly circ. 28,610.

Jones Jones & Jones
strategic marketers

MARKET:　　　Catalog Houses

RECOMMENDED ADVERTISING TYPE:　Print Space/Direct Mail/ Direct Sale (as private labels)

FREQUENCY:　Mixed

Pocket Analysis: As noted previously private labeling is a reality with **Clara's Classy Cookies**. Clara offers quality, competitive cost (to catalog houses), competitive pricing (to consumers), fast drop ship fulfillment and delivery, private label printing and assembly, a "no questions asked," money back or replacement refund policy, willingness to aid with special promotions, etc.

Direct mail is to be used as the ice-breaker, followed by direct sale from **Clara's Classy Cookies** internal sales staff. Advertising here is an explanatory vehicle and full color, full pages plus an introductory full-color double-page spread should be employed in appropriate business-to-business print publications.

1. Private Label Products & Services International: monthly circ. 22,460.

2. Private Brands World Book: annual circ. 22,755.

3. Key Branding & Private Label Weekly: weekly circ. 11,107.

Jones Jones & Jones
strategic marketers

ADDITIONAL ADVERTISING

Much is dependent on where and when we open accounts. Let's assume for example, as a result of our advertising in private label publications, or as a result of direct contacts, there is interest in **Clara's Classy Cookies** from supermarket chains. As a private label for Joe's Markets, a chain of 16 stores, we can supply certain lines. Promotion will be necessary. This will entail ads in local media (print, possibly radio or local TV), coupons (in-store and in-print media) as well as point-of-purchase displays. Jones, Jones & Jones can and will address these potentialities as they arise. We cannot advise a contingency fund for this purpose at this point.

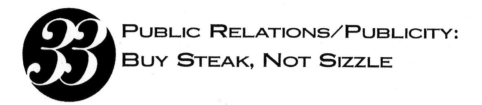

PUBLIC RELATIONS/PUBLICITY:
BUY STEAK, NOT SIZZLE

Public Relations:
Buy Steak, Not Sizzle

"Publicity, inasmuch as it is presented as a news story or feature article and not as an identifiable attempt to sell goods, services, or ideas, is more readily believed than advertising. Furthermore, studies have shown that publicity often attracts more reader attention than advertising, even when both appear on the same page."

S.M. ULANOFF
Advertising in America

Publicity is an excellent, cost-effective lead-generator and field exploration vehicle that should be used as often as possible. Basically it does six things:

1. Establishes a product position.

2. Moves the product/service, producing immediate sales.

3. Serves the primary function of informing large audiences at minimal costs.

4. Functions as a mini-marketing survey.

5. Sets the stage for future purchasing, via delayed recognition.

6. Enhances corporate image recognition.

It's no secret that public relations activities work. It's also no secret that it's not so much **what** you know, but **who** you know. And how well. And what the nature of that relationship is...and will be. With publicity, how dedicated and how well wired you are is often in direct ratio to how successful the program can become.

Quite a few things come together to compose an effective public relations program: scheduling, contact, fulfillment, editorial conferencing, the exquisiteness of timing a pseudo event, follow-up, etc. What Jones, Jones & Jones elected to do was based on timing, product and company development, budget, etc.

Jones Jones & Jones
strategic marketers

Examining Clara's Needs

We recognize that publicity/public relations are vital to the successful launch of **Clara's** the mail order company, **Clara's** the essential product line...and **Clara's** the future. However, as a strategic marketing organization, we recognize the fulcrum to be timing. In other words, **Clara's** may not be ready for the full gamut of publicity services. The following is what we feel **Clara's** will require in the next 12 months, barring any unforeseen circumstances.

(A) Press Release Generation:

To paraphrase Mr. Ulanoff, the press release is truly believability personified. Nothing works harder than good, solid, explicitly written press releases. However, **Clara's** needs a master cataloging of product/service "angles, hooks, tags, positions, raisons d'etre," etc., and a massive infusion of this type of placement activity. The more the merrier, as often as possible, to every potential source.

(B) Article Generation and Placement:

Articles are the most believable (and most believed) form of mass communication. **Clara's** needs as much of this exposure as possible. We are not necessarily advocates of the so-called "star vehicle approach," which we feel can be dehumanizing and will take Clara away from what she does best. However, it is vital that the leaders of our company, particularly Clara, are revealed to the trade, and established as legitimate thinkers/entrepreneurs/ spokesmen/gurus. We will create opportunities to launch photos, blurbs, articles, etc., involving our people. If this seems incongruous with our thought on the "star vehicle approach," suffice it to say that we believe in mass exposure, but unlike John Lennon, we do not believe that "any publicity is good publicity."

Jones Jones & Jones
strategic marketers

Jones, Jones & Jones Publicity Services

Publicity Program

This is designed to give **Clara's** full representation at all times, with complete coverage from start to finish. Jones, Jones & Jones' services herein include in no particular order:

A) assignment of an editorial supervisor and detail person for follow-up.

B) editorial contact and follow-up.

C) complete guidance on all publicity/P.R. matters involving product, company, personalities, etc.

D) article determination, conception, writing, and editing.

E) coordination of press releases (i.e., photography, interviews, printing, etc.).

F) concept through completion in crafting of customized releases and articles.

G) dissemination of press releases.

H) regular reporting to client.

I) coordination with sales force (if desired).

J) fulfillment.

Costs not included are photography, prints, and tax. Suggested monthly retainer cost: $5,000.

Our services are complete. In addition to several experienced writers who have a wealth of contacts in the marketplace, we also have on staff an accomplished editor. He is Mr. Joseph Jones (see résumé section) who spent ten years on the side of the coin we're aiming at. If anyone knows how to reach and influence editors...it is an editor himself.

Jones Jones & Jones

strategic marketers

SAMPLE PUBLICITY LIST

American Food & Beverage Honchos
Bake It Right
Bake 'N' Shake World
Bake Shop Business
Bakery News & Developments
Baking for Dollars
Brownie & Blondie Review
Chocochip News
Chocoholic World
Chocolate World News Review
Consumption
Cookie & Catalog World
Cookie Biz
Cookie Crumbles Register
Cookies, Cakes & Pies
Cookies! Cookies! Cookies!
Crumbs
Hotel Noshers Management
International Dough 'N' Spice
Journal of Professional Baking
Key Branding & Private Label Weekly
Motel Food Industry
New York Cookie Retailer
Ovens Galore
Private Brands World Book
Private Label Products & Services International
Reservations Please
Room Service Weekly
Taste Treats
U.S. Cookie Review
Women's Home Bakery

Furthermore...

You've seen all the interactive presentations you'll ever want to see...along with the completely tailored and coordinated posters, wind-up promotional items, caps, T-shirts, etc., that simply **MUST** go together. These items are termed sizzle. Steak involves hard work and it's something your SMO is far more likely to push rather than the former items.

1. Strategic Marketing and Publicity Plan Coordination

A strategic public relations plan begins with the identification of objectives of the company as a whole, as well as product/service marketing objectives. It examines the company's current situation in terms of product or service competition, market position (or lack of), distribution, and goals. The plan should clearly state program objectives and lay out strategies and tactics for achieving them. The plan must specify the target audiences, list tactics that support the strategies and objectives and will reach the target audiences effectively. It must specify timing and budget.

A good PR plan is both a map and a benchmark. Though it can (and should) evolve over time to meet changing market conditions, it points out the direction for client and agency, and at the end of the given period, the plan can evaluate whether or not the PR program has accomplished all that it promised.

2. Day-to-Day Mailing List

Mailing lists are boring. But a poor mailing list can torpedo a good PR program as surely as, well a torpedo. Some agencies rely on "canned" lists provided by mailing houses or clipping services. These are rarely, with notable exceptions, up-to-date, because the editorial community changes so rapidly.

Personalization is vital. Never use a media list wherein the listings are addressed to "the Editor." Any SMO can tell you editors do not generally appreciate this. Often the mailer winds up with a clerical person...or in the circular file. Leave list generation to the SMO. Let them determine which publications are correct for the company and the product or service. Let them get on the phone and get to know the correct editor(s).

3. Editorial Calendar Development

Meeting the objectives of an annual calendar of special subjects, topics, and issues for each medium isn't easy. It requires a lot of diligent effort. **Clara's** must be included in all relevant surveys, articles, once-overs, listings, and special issues.

Jones, Jones & Jones compiled a targeted editorial calendar that included some 56 consumer publications, 70 trade publications, eight independent newsletters, and numerous radio/TV stations. The master list condenses and cross-references all relevant issues and items in one document.

34 KEY COLLATERAL

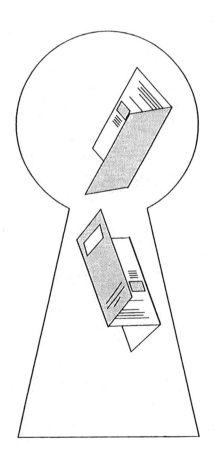

The SMO put together a sliding collateral plan, i.e., one dependent on manufacturing capability at a certain period in time. Essentially here is what pertained to **Clara's Classy Cookies**.

NUTRITIONAL BREAKDOWN CARDS

Cards such as these are important items to be used in every step of the marketing process. Consumers, retailers, salespeople all need to know the true facts about **Clara's Classy Cookies**...that they are made with 100% pure natural ingredients, in small batches (by commercial standards). Also vital is that in the specialty items line (e.g., dietetic, fat-free, etc.) the cookies deliver precisely what they promise. Nutritional breakdown "cards" inserted in every package, mailing carton, mail order tin, etc., can go a long way toward assuring our entire audience that they are paying for — and getting — nothing less than the best. We recommend color-coordinated "slips" 1.5″ x 3.5″ on a grainy (not pebbly!) stock, printed in one contrasting PMS color.

MISSION & PURPOSE STATEMENT

This will be an institutional item, one that "sets policy in a non-policy format." It must be to the point, authoritative, and handsome. A brief but "classy" 11″ x 17″, this is intended for external distribution to everyone from consumers to retailers to distributors to investment bankers. It will explain how we are in business, why we are in business, and whom we are in business to reach and support. It can be as extensive as we like; it should be used as a guide at all times, by reps on sales calls, in binders with all our sales forms, at sales presentations, etc.

Jones Jones & Jones
strategic marketers

PRODUCT SALES PRIMERS

Since salespeople and telemarketers are the essential vanguard in our promotion...we must have excellent communication with them...and provide campaign rationale and strategy...long before any **Clara's Classy Cookies** campaign breaks. This guide is an instructional summary piece that will fit the bill. This need not be a fancy or expensive piece; the point is to be informative and easy to absorb. This is for our sales related people only...not for customers or distributors, retailers, etc. "Why?" you might ask...because we need to have the sales force behind us and behind the program at all times...following the thematic approach established by marketing...before the customer sees our campaign. This is the piece to explain why...how...who...what...and where...to our people who need to know what to expect and what to say...to the people who will eventually buy our products, and company. Content is vital...to unify our sales effort in every detail. The piece will not tell the sales force how to sell...they already know that...but it will discuss and direct their attention to various parts of the campaign.

MISCELLANEOUS CONTINGENCY

We are aware that the extraordinary demands of a start-up operation will flurry and halt, start and stop, come and go. It's never too early to anticipate that we may need, for example, **Clara's Classy Cookies** line cards, promotional items, videos, etc. As of now, we can only speculate on what unique demands the consumer and reseller markets will make; therefore, we have reserved a contingency fund until those demands begin to clarify themselves.

Jones Jones & Jones
strategic marketers

CAPABILITIES AND FACILITIES BROCHURE SYSTEM

The need for such a piece exists to identify **Clara's Classy Cookies** to our target audiences, particularly those segments that do not know us. We need to establish who we are, what it is that we do, and above all, how well we do it. Many organizations have two separate pieces, one for facilities, a second for capabilities. We recommend combination of capability, facility, and identity in one piece; the rationale is purely budgetary. We also recommend incorporating this in a pocket folder with an insert sheet system for added utilization.

The Need for Modularity:

We see the most cost-effective design for multi-function collateral material as a 9″ x 12″ pocket folder. This will enable **Clara's Classy Cookies** to custom design promotional efforts for each prospective market, customer, etc., on an individual basis; so the right package is used with the right prospect. **Clara's Classy Cookies'** "best foot" is always forward.

Resource Dedication:

The modular folder itself contains all pertinent information that does not readily change. It will function as a mini-facilities piece. Reprinting brochures is expensive and certainly the last thing we wish to do with a limited budget. Items such as corporate statements, philosophy, departments, etc., are intended for placement in the folder. Photos or illustrations, real or ideal, can also be incorporated as needed. Individual sheets can be generated for each capability...updated singularly as needed...giving us strong fiscal conservation.

Jones Jones & Jones
strategic marketers

Suffice it to say that such a comprehensive message delivery system is targeted to do the following:

1. Inform new audiences of the availability and depth of our products, support, and services.

2. Be a "ready-reference" for our existing customers.

3. Have the capability to be used by salespeople/customer service personnel, etc., in face-to-face presentations, sales calls, over the telephone, etc.

4. Be versatile in use and in production/dissemination economy.

5. Be desirable to read, easy to understand, and simple to recall.

6. Be available to be used in non-marketing presentations, where deemed desirable.

7. Represent **Clara's Classy Cookies** in the most accurate, most professional, most unilaterally beneficial manner.

8. Be able to be used in response to all inquiries...telemarketing, ads, direct mail, at trade shows, etc.

35 DIRECT MAIL, NOT SO DIRECTLY

Direct Mail

Direct mail did not immediately figure into Jones, Jones & Jones' plan in a big way. However, to accelerate activity at a few trade shows, particularly the PLPB Show in June, the SMO recognized that pre-show direct mail to registered attendees could make a huge difference. Also targeted were catalog houses, hotels, and eventually specific consumers. However, this was deemed overly ambitious for **Clara's** first year and a budget was recommended only for the first mentioned pre-show mailer.

WHY USE DIRECT MAIL?

Why not? Direct mail is a promotional vehicle that provides a dedicated, **personalized** market approach, one that enhances and capitalizes on our print space campaign.

More specifically, direct mail allows **Clara's Classy Cookies** to select specific features/benefits, and show the targeted audience how these features/benefits fulfill their requirements.

Direct mail is an effective inquiry producer that gives us **CONTROL**. We decide **WHO** gets the mailing, **WHEN** they get it, and **WHAT** format they'll receive. As far as **WHO** is concerned, we never pay for unwanted audiences, which makes direct mail extremely cost-effective. As for **WHEN,** direct mail timing is completely controlled by us, guaranteeing the best hit dates and immediacy of action. The **WHAT** aspect is easily seen in the format used, the information contained, and the manner of audience response. Most of all, direct mail gives us promotional flexibility.

Each **Clara's** mailer should primarily isolate and focus on a concrete message of interest to the reader, in this case trade show focus. This gives the mailer a justifiable reason for existing, in the opinion of our audience, and makes it easier for us to monitor and track needs/interests. Headline and captions command attention. Body copy expands on that message and succinctly ties it into one or more of our applicable market themes.

Size

There are no ironclad guidelines for the size of a direct mail piece. Size is more often determined by direction, message, volume of information, function, postal requirements, and other factors. Since direct mail must be fresh, interesting, and attention-getting if it is to be read, we insist on total flexibility regarding size. This affords us unlimited freedom for necessary innovations.

Content

Content must be geared to the receiving audience. **THIS IS VITALLY TRUE IN OUR AREA.** Never assume a great ad (i.e., ad reprints) will make a great direct mailer. That's a common mistake. Great **DIRECTION** (message, graphics, etc.) makes a great direct mailer. Our content will have superb direction and be informative, instructive, reassuring, and above all, interesting. Dull direct mail pieces, however well-directed, NEVER get the attention of those that are ALSO entertaining. Let our readers LOOK FORWARD to each piece we send. **"OKAY, WHAT'S CLARA'S UP TO NOW?"**

Impact

Direct mail, by its nature, is immediate but short-lived. **Clara's** direct mail pieces will immediately grab the reader's attention and prompt them to action. The biggest mistake one can make is the pompous assumption that the target audience wants to be disturbed by your "vital" message...especially during a busy day. Size, color, message, and other factors have been selected with this in mind, incorporated graphically into attention-getting design and copy that: a) gets our direct mailers past the screening eyes of secretaries, etc., and into the hands of our targets; and b) makes our direct mailers worth the valuable time our target audiences will devote to them.

Jones Jones & Jones
strategic marketers

Mailer vs. Self-Mailer

We like the use of self-mailing direct mail pieces, which require no envelopes, wherever possible. This saves time and dollars and allows for immediate message impact on our audiences. However, due to the nature of our particular recommended mailing, we must use standard mailer-in-envelopes. We also recommend the use of detachable business reply cards, postage paid, to facilitate quick, easy response from interested prospects.

Color

Again, flexibility is a key. The purpose, intent, and content of each individual piece normally determines color requirements. We anticipate the use of two colors for our products. This will make maximum use of our budgetary dollars.

Jones Jones & Jones
strategic marketers

RECOMMENDED DIRECT MAIL PROGRAM

We recommend the inclusion of pre-trade show direct mail to the attendees of the PLPB (Private Label/Private Brand Show) in June. The mailer should invite the attendee to stop by for free cookies and any one of the delicacy coffees... Jamaican Blue Mountain, Kona, etc., as well as teas and other beverages. The invitation should be specific for a line of cookies. We suggest selecting four main products (i.e., Academia Nut, Gigando Hodgepodge, Strawberry Yummies, and the ever-popular Chocolate Razzmatazz) and dividing the mailing list of 16,000 attendees by product, 4,000 mailings of each. To enhance the attractiveness of our products, we recommend using microencapsulation.

Microencapsulation

Nothing sells cookies like the aroma of fresh baked products. Whether it's the savory scent of cinnamon, cloves, ginger, and allspice...the sweetness of nutmeg and mace, the scintillation of vanilla, the promise of peanut butter, the tang of orange, lemon, and citrus, scent is certainly a powerful enticer. Scent, combined with mouth-watering photography or sensuous illustrations is very difficult to resist. The instant the mailer is opened, scent will bombard the recipient. Our mailers will reach our audiences creating a powerful message by their appearance and aroma: that **Clara's Classy Cookies** are "world class products, available for private labeling. See us at booth #1234."

36 PACKAGE DESIGN

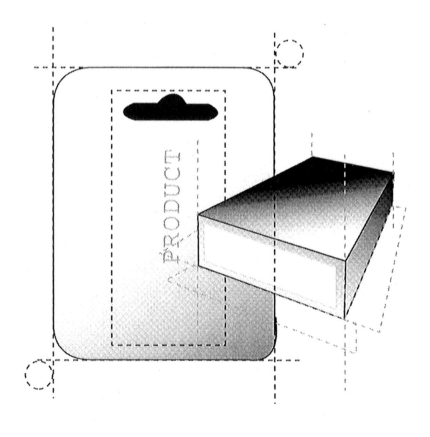

PRODUCT

Packaging became a major element in **Clara's** budgetary allotment. Several items, e.g., various sized tins and the like would not be ready the first year (at least unless a huge order was forthcoming!). The SMO's recommendations focused on the first year's realities.

Jones Jones & Jones
strategic marketers

Color, feel, quality, eye appeal, and design are all large elements of package design. While we have limited the number of designs by virtue of modularity, a production budget ensues. Printing of such packages is as yet undetermined due to fast increasing orders. A proper print budget will be determined when **Clara's** is comfortable with order numbers.

37 BUDGETS AND SCHEDULES TIME AGAIN

Isn't it truly astonishing that no matter what avenue(s) are pursued, you always wind up at the budget page? Well, it shouldn't be astonishing you by this point. No SMO can exist without a budget...or for very long with a poorly designed, or appropriated one. So grab the bull by the horns, plug into real-time, and make sure your budgets are both accurate and flexible. It's not impossible, it just seems that way. Jones, Jones & Jones put it all together for **Clara's** and the bottom line was actually pretty reasonable.

Jones, Jones & Jones, Strategic Marketers, 1234 Main Street
Carbuncle, IA 45678 • Tel: (444) 444-4444 • Fax: (444) 444-4445

CLARA'S CLASSY COOKIES

MEDIA SCHEDULE — JANUARY - DECEMBER (page 1 of 2)

PUBLICATION	JAN	FEB	MAR	APR	MAY	JUN	JUL	AUG	SEP	OCT	NOV	DEC
Bake 'N' Shake World 6X $3,030	1		2		3		4		5		6	
Cookie Crumbles Register 6X $3,690		1		2		3		4		5		6
Bake Shop Business 6X $3,215	1		2		3		4		5		6	
Reservations Please 18X $4,460	1/2	3	4/5	6	7/8	9	10/11	12	13/14	15	16/17	18
Room Service Weekly 18X $4,055	1/2	3	4/5	6	7/8	9	10/11	12	13/14	15	16/17	18
HNM 6X $4,650	1			2		3		4		5		6
American Food & Beverage Honchos 18X $2,520	1	2/3	4	5/6	7	8/9	10	11/12	13	14/15	16	17/18

TOTAL EXPENDITURE (page 1) = $286,140.00

Jones, Jones & Jones, Strategic Marketers, 1234 Main Street
Carbuncle, IA 45678 • Tel: (444) 444-4444 • Fax: (444) 444-4445

CLARA'S CLASSY COOKIES

MEDIA SCHEDULE — JANUARY - DECEMBER (page 2 of 2)

PUBLICATION	JAN	FEB	MAR	APR	MAY	JUN	JUL	AUG	SEP	OCT	NOV	DEC
Private Brands World Book 12X $5,710	1	2	3	4	5	6	7	8	9	10	11	12
Private Brands World Book Annual 1X $6,110			1									
Key Branding & Private Label Weekly 9x $3,880	1		2	3	4	5	6		7		8	9
Private Label Products & Services Intl. 6X $4,315		1		2		3		4		5		6

TOTAL EXPENDITURE (page 2) = $135,440.00

GRAND TOTAL MEDIA EXPENDITURE = $271,580.00

strategic marketers

BUDGETS AND SCHEDULES

ELEMENT I: 1995 NEWSLETTER PRODUCTION

Complete production of 24-page, five-color self-mailing newsletter with business reply card, Volume 1, Number 1 including concept, layout, design, copy, typography, art, photography, retouching, stats, computer mechanical (per issue $32,500.00).

12 original issues 1995   **$390,000.00**

ELEMENT II: 1995 NEWSLETTER PRINTING

24 pages, five-color, including stock, bindery, varnish, saddle stitching, die-cutting, etc., 50,000-75,000 pcs.

12 issues @ $22,612.00   **$271,344.00**

Fulfillment
Addressing, labeling, mailing

12 issues @ $8,000.00   **$ 96,000.00**

ELEMENT III: LIST ACQUISITION

50,000-75,000 fully culled names   **$ 12,760.00**

ELEMENT IV: LIST MAINTENANCE

Average cost per month, 12 @ $1,000.00   **$ 12,000.00**

Jones Jones & Jones
strategic marketers

ELEMENT V: LOGO DEVELOPMENT AND DESIGN

a) **Clara's Classy Cookies**

b) **Clara's Classy Cookies** with subsets for each individual product (Snackerino Almond, Strawberry Yummies, Chocolate Razzmatazz, Academia Nut, Vanilla Wholly Molie, Pineapple Princesses w/ Academia Nuts, Space Spice 'n' Raisin)

c) **Clara's Classy Cookies** with subsets for product category and individual product:
- Oversized Cookies (1)
- Fat-Free (2)
- Dietetic (2)
- Hi-Cal (2)

TOTAL	**$ 28,500.00**

ELEMENT VI: TASTE TEST BUDGET

$ 85,000.00

ELEMENT VII: KEY FOCUS GROUP

$ N/A

ELEMENT VIII: TRIAL BALLOON TELEMARKETING

$ 75,000.00

ELEMENT IX: TRADE SHOW BOOTH DESIGN AND CONSTRUCTION

$ 45,000.00

ELEMENT X: SUPPORT ADVERTISING

Bakery Segment

a) Bake 'N' Shake World, full page, 4c: **$ 18,180.00**
   6X @ $3,030 =

b) Cookie Crumbles Register, full page, 4c: **$ 22,140.00**
   6X @ $3,690 =

c) Bake Shop Business, full page, 4c: **$ 19,290.00**
   6X @ $3,215 =   **SUBTOTAL**   **$ 59,610.00**

ELEMENT X: SUPPORT ADVERTISING (con't)
Hotel Segment

a) Reservations Please, full page, 4c:
   18X @ $4,460 = $ 80,280.00
b) Room Service Weekly, full page, 4c:
   18X @ $4,055 = $ 72,990.00
c) HNM, full page, 4c:
   6X @ $4,650 = $ 27,900.00
                              SUB TOTAL   **$181,170.00**

Catalog Houses

a) Private Brands World Book, full page, 4c:
   12X @ $5,710 = $ 68,520.00
b) Key Branding & Private Label Weekly, full page, 4c:
   9X @ $3,880 = $ 34,920.00
c) Private Brands World Book, Annual, full
   page, 4c:
   1X @ $6,110 = $ 6,110.00
d) Private Label Products & Services Intl., full page, 4c:
   6X @ $4,315 = $ 25,890.00
                              SUB TOTAL   **$135,440.00**

ELEMENT XI: PUBLIC RELATIONS
Retainer Basis: $5,000 per month, 12 months $ 60,000.00

Jones Jones & Jones
strategic marketers

ELEMENT XII: KEY COLLATERAL

a) Nutritional Breakdown Cards, 1c, 500,000 pcs. $ 12,500.00
    print and production
b) Mission Statement, 100,000 pcs. $ 15,000.00
    print and production
c) Product Sales Primers, 2,000 pcs. $ 4,400.00
    print and production $ 10,000.00
d) Contingency   **SUB TOTAL**   **$ 41,900.00**

ELEMENT XIII: CAPABILITIES/FACILITIES BROCHURE

Capabilities/Facilities Brochure, 5,000 pcs. $ 25,000.00
print and production

ELEMENT XIV: DIRECT MAIL

Production, printing, microencapsulation of $ 44,750.00
16,000 pcs.

ELEMENT XV: PACKAGE DESIGN

•**Clara's Classy Cookies** 3 oz., 6 oz., 1 lb., 2 lb., 3 lb.
•**Clara's Classy Cookies** 3 oz. packages and 11 oz. packages
subsets for Snakerino Almond, Strawberry Yummies, Chocolate
Razzmatazz, Academia Nut, Vanilla Wholly Molie, Pineapple
Princesses w/Academia Nuts, Space Spice 'n' Raisin

•**Clara's Classy Cookies:**
    •Oversized Cookies (1) 3 oz., 6 oz., 12 oz.
    •Fat-Free (2) 3 oz., 16 oz., 22 oz.
    •Dietetic (2) 3 oz., 16 oz., 22 oz.
    •Hi-Cal (2) 3 oz., 16 oz., 22 oz.

    Clara's 1 lb. assortment
    Clara's 2 lb. assortment
    Clara's 5 lb. assortment
                                                          $70,000.00

Budget

 # BEFORE WE SAY GOODNIGHT...

It's 10 o'clock. Do you know where your SMO is?

After taking an in-depth look at SMOs for a few hundred pages, wouldn't it be nice to have an abbreviated, short-form, top-to-bottom, A to Z, no bull, facts-only overview of our subject? Here it is. And though it loses something in the contracting, here are six key defining points to keep in mind about SMOs at all times:

(1) The major difference between SMOs and all other marketing-related organizations is one of attitude. SMOs regard the organizations they represent as clients...not as accounts.

(2) The SMOs recognize that the proliferation of the client's business is of paramount import. Without the client's business, there would be no business for the SMO. The SMO recognizes this relationship and actively promotes it.

(3) The SMO provides the research and development, the strategic, tactical, and creative plans...and implements them all.

(4) The SMO is structured to provide services for a long business relationship, rather than hit and run short-term tactics.

(5) With a competent SMO working directly with (or without) an internal marketing department, clients are free to concentrate on their core businesses.

(6) The SMO is active in all five areas:
a) research.
b) strategic marketing.
c) creative endeavors.
d) tactical marketing.
e) implementation.

Could we list 25 or more factors? Of course. Would that make sense? No, because that might prevent some people from reading the whole book and absorbing the whole story. And since the SMO is such a conceptual composite of finite and infinite marketing strategies, the many nuances and niches should never be overlooked.

Using the services of an SMO can make a huge difference in the success of virtually any business. Whether you are an organization such as **Clara's Classy Cookies** or *Frimmels Are Us*...whether you're privately held, publicly owned, Mom and Pop, or multinational, really doesn't enter the equation. To harvest the benefits of an SMO and truly get the most from your budget, your mindset/attitude/outlook/philosophy has to be open, honest, and realistic. Arm yourself with this, go out and get that strategic marketing organization, play your own role in developing and implementing a successful, goal-oriented program...and enjoy the prosperity.

BIBLIOGRAPHY

Andrew, Bryan. *Creative Product Development: A Marketing Approach to New Product Innovation.* ©1975. Dingman.

Bernstein, Charles. *Sambos: Only a Fraction of the Action.* ©1984. Burbank, CA: National Literary Guild, Inc.

Buell, Victor P., editor. *Handbook of Modern Marketing.* 1986. McGraw-Hill.

Buskirk, Richard. *Principles of Marketing.* 1970. Holt, Rinehart and Winston.

Canon U.S.A., Inc. *Newslink,* Volume 6, No. 2. 1994. Office Equipment Service Division.

Chajet, Clive, and Shachtman, Tom. *Image by Design: From Corporate Vision to Business Reality.* 1991. Addison-Wesley.

Davidson, Jeff. *Marketing on a Shoestring.* ©1994. Wiley.

Engle, James F., Wales, Hugh G., and Warshaw, Martin P. *Promotional Strategy.* ©1975. R.D. Irwin.

Frank R.E., Massey, Wm. F., and Wind, Yoram. *Market Segmentation.* ©1972. Prentice-Hall.

Graphic Design: USA. Volume 30, No. 10. October 1994. Kaye Publishing Corporation.

Holtz, H.R. *Secrets of Practical Marketing for Small Business.* ©1982. Prentice-Hall.

Iacocca, Lee with Novak, William. *Iacocca.* ©1984 by Lee Iacocca. Bantam Books, Inc.

Katsaros, John. *Selling High Tech High Ticket.* ©1993. Probus Publishing Company.

Kawasaki, Guy. *Selling the Dream.* ©1991. Harper Business 1992.

Levinson, J.C. *Guerilla Marketing: Secrets for Making Big Profits from Your Small Business.* 1993. Houghton Mifflin.

McKay, E.S. *The Marketing Mystique.* ©1972. American Management Association.

McKenna, Regis. *The Regis Touch.* ©1985. Addison-Wesley Publishing Company, Inc.

McQuail, Denis. *Sociology of Mass Communications.* ©1972. Penguin Books, Ltd.

Margrath, Allan J. *The 6 Imperatives of Marketing.* 1992. Amacom: American Management Assn.

Matthews, Jack L. *Sales Driven: Turning Your Company into a Marketing Machine.* ©1993. Probus Publishing Company.

Mitchell, Gary. *The Heart of the Sale: Making the Customer Need to Buy. The Key to Successful Selling.* ©1991. Amacom.

Nichols, Judith E. *By the Numbers: Using Demographics and Psychographics for Business Growth in the 90's.* ©1990. Bonus Books.

Quest for Prosperity. 1988. PHP Institute, Inc.

Stanton, William J. and Futrell, Charles. *Fundamentals of Marketing.* ©1987. McGraw-Hill Book Company.

Wedell, E.G. *Broadcasting and Public Policy.* ©1968. Joseph.

Index